ZEN
GARDENING

ZEN GARDENING

SUNNIVA HARTE

PAVILION

First published in Great Britain in 1999 by
Pavilion Books Limited
London House, Great Eastern Wharf, Parkgate Road,
London SW11 4NQ

Text © Sunniva Harte 1999
The moral right of the author has been asserted.

Picture credits given on page 160.

Designed by Andrew Barron &
Collis Clements Associates
Picture research by Emily Hedges

A CIP catalogue record for this book is available from
the British Library

1 86205 152 6

Typeset in Geometric

Colour reproduction by DP Graphics
Printed and bound in Singapore by Imago

10 9 8 7 6 5 4 3 2 1

This book may be ordered by post direct from the
publisher. Please contact the Marketing Department
but try your bookshop first.

CONTENTS

54

Rocks & stones
Creating space
and energy

6

Introduction

74

Sand & gravel
Creating simplicity
and serenity

14

**Elements & their
symbolism**
The principles of
Zen gardening

94

Plants
Creating harmony
and profusion

114

**Architectural
elements**
Creating views
and focal points

156

Glossary and
Bibliography

157

Index

34

Water
Creating balance
and tranquillity

136

Ornaments
Creating interest
and beauty

160

Acknowledgements

Opposite:
Naturally weathered
rocks and carefully
raked sand evoke a
feeling of calmness
typical of Zen
gardens.

Do not seek to follow in the

footsteps of the Masters; seek

what they sought.

Zen saying

INTRODUCTION

It seems that now, more than ever, people are trying especially hard to make their busy lives less stressful and more meaningful. Gardening can help in a subtle way that few other activities can manage, and I believe that the guiding principles of Zen gardening can lead to the creation of a truly calming, harmonious and uplifting environment. These gardens are not designed to excite the senses as Western plots do but are places where the spirit has peace and tranquillity in which to grow. Zen Buddhism requires that every task is performed with love – and it is the love and care that is put into them that gives them a serene and kindly atmosphere. 'Zen' means meditation, and gardens that have been designed along Zen principles are places where contemplation and meditation are possible.

Zen gardening was, and still is, practised by Buddhist monks in Japan. Following

Zen gardens come in different guises: they can be green and verdant, evoking an ancient, unspoilt wood; they can also be starkly abstract, resembling a painting whose challenging use of space provokes new thoughts. Although I have not studied Zen gardening with a master gardener, I can, with my photographer's eye, my knowledge of gardening and my concern for the well-being of my fellow human beings, show how it is possible to recreate the essence of a Zen garden in a Western climate.

a strand of Buddhism known as Zen, they believe that contemplation and meditation are vital tools in the quest for self-knowledge. Buddha himself searched long and hard for the meaning of life and finally achieved enlightenment seated under a tree. This event is what all Zen practitioners seek to achieve in their own lives. Their gardens are therefore designed to be soothing and reflective spaces that remain visually the same from one year to another. Zen uses riddles, known as koans, to break through conventional thought so as to help students discover the meaning of life. In practising Zen, it is important to have the correct posture when walking and sitting. Zen gardens accommodate all these needs, which is why they always feel gentle, spiritual and unworldly. The unique style of Zen gardens ensures that by using rocks and plants in both a symbolic and natural way, and by devising pathways that require care when walking on, the visitor unwittingly follows Zen ways.

It is important to understand that we in the West have different intellectual and emotional starting points from the Japanese or Chinese. For example, a Japanese child will not equate harmony in design with even numbers or pairs – if asked to create a harmonious pattern, he will make an asymmetrical design, whereas a western child will make a symmetrical one. Similarly, in Zen gardening asymmetrical designs are seen as closer to the natural order of things than symmetrical compositions. Plants and objects arranged in odd numbers create a subtle calmness and have a greater sense of balance in a garden.

The Japanese tend to value aspects of the natural world that westerners consider pleasant but of no great importance. In spring, for example, Japanese television broadcasts daily bulletins on the flowering of blossom trees. Pilgrimages are made to view the blossom and appreciate the qualities of each tree as it heralds the approach of warmer weather; journeys are made into the countryside to gaze

at scenic views bathed in the magical silver light of a full moon.

The desire to view natural scenes collectively goes back to the days when Shintō was the prevailing religion in Japan. Shrines were built of simple plant material and usually placed in beautiful surroundings. The spirits of animals and other natural living things were honoured. There were no written texts, and worship took the form of silent contemplation. Water became a vital element in purification rituals, while revered trees or rocks were encircled with rope and the ground around them covered in white gravel to denote a holy area.

When Buddhism was brought to Japan from China via Korea in the sixth century, the Japanese people were already predisposed towards a religious culture that laid great emphasis on meditation, the simplicity of building design and the power of the natural world. The Japanese admired the Chinese civilization and tried to emulate it.

In AD 794, during the Heian period (794–1185), the capital of Japan was moved from Nara to Heian-Kyo (Kyōto), known as the Capital of Peace and Tranquillity. It was during this time that the Chinese science of geomancy, or Feng Shui, was introduced. Exponents of geomancy believe that there are unseen natural forces at work all around us. These forces are Yin and Yang, the negative and the positive, or female and male, which can be influenced by judicious landscaping or building. During the Heian period, nobles vied with each other to create beautiful gardens along these lines, which could be viewed either from a boat or on foot.

The design of gardens was based on a mixture of beliefs and ideas that were compatible with each other. Geomancy decreed that streams and rivers ran from east to west to create an environment that felt balanced, Shintō required large rocks to be incorporated into the overall design, and Amida Buddhist ideas (see p. 18) introduced 'paradise islands', reminders that it was possible to break out of the endless cycle of rebirth and reside in paradise (see p. 18).

There is scant documented evidence of when or where the first Zen garden was made, whether in China or Japan. It is known that the temple Kenchōji, now referred to as Tokōji, was founded in 1253 during the Kamakura period (1185–1333), by Rankei Doryu, who practised Pure Zen, a strict form of Buddhism imported from China. Although nothing remains of the temple's first garden, we know that it was a contemplative garden, which was viewed

see p. 18

Below:
At Ryōanji, sand has been used to mimic rapidly flowing water to contrast with the limpid pool close by.

Opposite:
**The rich autumn tints
of mosses and acers
are perfectly framed
by the open door,
allowing those within
the building full
enjoyment of the
garden.**

in formal arrangements that were meant to represent certain Buddhist philosophical formulations, to help his students to a direct, intuitive realization of the truth behind these abstract ideas.

The Japanese are adept at grasping abstract ideas. An open mind and a clear heart are necessary for understanding a Japanese garden, so that the imagination can come into play when interpreting the significance of a waterfall, rock grouping or island construction.

from inside a nearby building. It also had a central pond in the Chinese style. Today, the temple is famous for its Chinese-style landscape and dragon-shaped pond.

The greatest of the Zen garden masters during the Kamakura period was Musō Sōseki (1275–1351). He was reputed to have had thousands of students and taught Five Mountain, or Gozan Buddhism, another strand of Buddhism from China that appealed to and was loyal to the ruling Shogunate. Ink painting was popular among Gozan priests and followed traditional lines and themes, which were then transposed into gardens. Musō Sōseki is thought to have developed Saihōji and Tenryūji in Kyōto. Saihōji has a Jōdo-style, or Pure Land (see p. 18) pond, which is now famous for growing more than 40 different types of moss. Tenryūji has a two-tier dry waterfall in the style of a Chinese ink painting, which is much admired today. Musō Sōseki was renowned for his great skill in rock placement; today, the positioning of rocks is still considered a great art. He devised ways of placing rocks

There were five different schools of Zen Buddhism imported from China. Each would have its own huge temple complexes that contained smaller temples and gardens within them. Here Buddhist priests lived with their families, since they were allowed to marry and have children. Once an Emperor retired he might well become a priest or at least found a temple such as Myoshinji or Daitokuji, which was founded by the Emperor Hanazono (1297–1348), who followed the most revered priests of the Pure Land at that time, Shuho Myocho and Kanzan Egen. At Myoshinji, there is an original dry water garden or *karesansui*, renowned for its moving arrangement of stones. One of the largest Zen temples in Japan, Myoshinji has had a lasting influence on Japanese garden styles. Daitokuji is famous for its wonderful collection of stones, in which a central rock representing Mount Sumeru, the mythical centre of the Buddhist world, is encircled by smaller rocks representing eight mountain ranges. This theme was a popular one and used in later garden designs.

The Muromachi period (1333–1573) saw a resurgence of Chinese influence on garden design derived from scroll paintings of mountainous scenery and ancient trees. The most powerful shogun of the time was Yoshimitsu (1358–1408), an admirer of Chinese art, who visited the temple garden of Saihōji to study how its rocks were perfectly arranged among the moss, to give it a mystical air in keeping with its Pure Land theme. Yoshimitsu had his own garden built with a fabulous Chinese-style pavilion – the Golden Pavilion. After his death, the garden became a Zen temple and is now known as Rokuonji. Developed over the centuries, Rokuonji set the tone for later Zen gardens. It has one of the most admired dragon-gate waterfalls, or *ryūmon*, as well as incorporating rocks symbolic of the Taoist mythology, Hōraito, and an arrangement of three stones known as *sanzon*, or Three Buddhas (see pp. 21–22).

originally developed as a way of helping monks maintain mindfulness while serving and drinking the tea they needed to stay awake during hours of meditation.

The ceremony created the right atmosphere in which to discuss art and play guessing games. The narrow area leading to the tea house, known as the *roji*, was planted and paved with great care to prepare the visitor spiritually for the ceremony. Much can be learnt from the attractively landscaped design of such a notoriously difficult area.

Opposite:
The varied leaf textures and colours of Hosta, Acer, Fatsia and Bamboo, together with the smooth pebbles and rough gravel create a visually exciting picture.

The Ōnin civil wars, which lasted from 1467 until 1469, devastated Japan. As most houses were built of light wood and thatch, they were easily destroyed by fire and, at the end of the fighting, half of Kyōto had been destroyed. The new Kyōto was greatly influenced by Zen priests who advocated *karesansui*, or dry rock gardening (see p. 22). Although *karesansui* had featured in earlier Zen temple gardens, the style was now perfected. White sand representing the ocean or 'no-mind' was raked into various designs. As large gardens became fabulously expensive to build and most garden plots were therefore reduced in size, simpler, abstract gardens in the *karesansui* style were greatly favoured.

The Momoyama (Peach Mountain) period (1573–1603) that followed was one of feudal strife. Buddhism became less influential, while the Chinese tea ceremony became increasingly popular. Although far from ostentatious, the tea ceremony was nevertheless able to convey in subtle ways the owner's taste and wealth. It was

In 1542, Portuguese sailors visited Japan, and it is believed that their tales of grand European castles inspired the building of the first Japanese castle in 1578. Large gardens were also built at this time, and at Juraku-dai a huge lake and artificial hill were constructed using stones and plants from gardens already established. This strategy continues today: the creation of many public Japanese gardens in the US has only been possible through the use of unwanted local paving, as at the Japanese garden in Portland, Oregon, US, or by the acquisition of suitable private plant collections, as at the Golden Gate Park in San Francisco.

There came a time of greater stability during the Edo period (1603–1868) when Japan became very introspective and was all but closed to the West. The development of gardens continued until the eighteenth century, but then began to stagnate because of the lack of external stimulation. When Japan reopened its ports to Western vessels in 1868, during the Meiji period, it created a surge of

excitement and interest in the West for anything oriental.

From the 1880s, many Japanese travelled to the west coast of America to settle and make their fortunes, taking their knowledge of Zen gardening with them. Since the end of the Second World War, most American cities have acquired a Japanese sister city. Together, the twinned cities have built Japanese gardens within an existing botanical or public garden. The healing power of garden-making has enabled these two great nations to look positively to the future. In Europe, wealthy individuals built Japanese gardens within a larger garden for their personal enjoyment and that of their friends.

Only when you have no thing

in your mind and no mind in things

are you vacant and spiritual,

empty and marvellous.

Te-shan/Tokusan, 780–865

Symbolism has become woven into the lives of the Japanese, enriching them deeply. To appreciate Zen gardens it is important to understand why and how the elements used in them came to be of importance to the Japanese. Symbolism is used widely in their temple gardens as a means of visually reminding the ordinary person of their place in the universe. With the use of

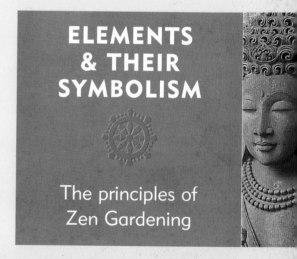

ELEMENTS & THEIR SYMBOLISM

The principles of Zen Gardening

rocks, sand and water the Japanese are shown their place in the natural order of the earth, which is both grounding and reassuring. At the same time an element of humour can be introduced into the garden, again through the use of symbolism.

The growth of symbolism Japan consists of a series of islands that lie close to Korea; its verdant mountains and clear, gushing streams have always commanded respect from its people.

Once Japan had become an agricultural country, greater importance was attached to its natural elements. Wet rice farming developed between 300 BC and AD 300, which necessitated the careful management of water in order to obtain the maximum yield. By the fifth and sixth centuries, Shintō, a religion that revered water, stones and other natural elements but had no written texts, had evolved.

The Japanese were very aware of how sophisticated China was in terms of lifestyle and education, and tried to emulate it from an early period. During the Heian period (794–1185), Chinese dress was worn at court and the art of poetry writing became a necessary accomplishment. Chinese Taoist thoughts on the meaning of life had begun to be incorporated into Buddhism in the third century AD and this melding of ideas was introduced to Japan. Here, it fused with Shintō beliefs, which continue to the present day. For example, parents will take new-born children to a Shintō ceremony of purification, since childbirth is considered unclean; those children will eventually have a Buddhist ceremony performed when a parent dies.

Both the Chinese and Japanese have always had a deep love of mountains and a belief that important mountains play a central role in the evolution of man. Fables associated with mountains were taken to the hearts of these peoples. It stands to reason that Chinese gardens and, later, Japanese gardens should emphasize the power of nature by incorporating representational mountains into their design.

The most influential fable concerned a group of five islands – P'eng-lai, Ying-chou, Fang-hu, Yuan-ch'iao and Tai-yu – that held the secret of immortal life. Known as the Mystic Isles of the Blest, they were believed to lie off the coast of Korea; tantalizingly, they vanished into a heavy mist whenever sailors approached them. The islands were reputed to be very beautiful, with steep mountains clothed in a marvellous variety of plant life. Trees were laden with precious stones, while their fruit, when eaten, gave the power of immortality. The birds and animals on the islands were symbolically white to signify purity (white animals were also prized in the West and believed to have special powers, and even today it is still considered bad luck to shoot a white pheasant, deer or fox). Gold and silver buildings were built on the terraced slopes of the mountains and in these lived the Immortals, or Hsien. Once ordinary people, they had in different ways achieved a state of perpetual youth, so that illness and ageing were unknown to them. Miraculously, they could fly or float through the air, although sometimes they travelled from island to island on the backs of huge cranes. By association with this myth, cranes came to represent longevity and were represented in gardens by a particular grouping of rocks (see p. 42).

(see p. 42).

The Hsien were able to live where they chose, although they usually stayed on their own Mystic Isles. At first the islands were not anchored to the seabed, and the Hsien grew disgruntled with their constant movement. After listening to their complaints, the Supreme Ruler of the Universe commanded 15 sea turtles to support the five islands on their backs, which is how turtles came to have a special place in Chinese and Japanese mythology, and to represent longevity.

Below:
Japanese cranes
representing longevity,
and a small pagoda
surrounded by grass,
add a mystical touch
to this verdant scene.

The tranquil lives of the Hsien were upset when a giant fished too close to the islands and inadvertently caught six of the sea turtles. Unsupported, the islands of Yuan-ch'iao and Tai-yu floated into the ocean mists, never to be seen again.

Man has always yearned for immortality, and the Emperor Wu of Han in China was no exception. He devised a plan to lure the Hsien away from their islands to his Chinese estate. Here he had a vast lake, in the centre of which was an island that rose majestically out of the water. On this and two other islands in the lake he had built palaces named after the three Mystic Isles. He hoped these would entice the flying Immortals to choose them as their abodes. Once the islands were inhabited by the Hsien, he imagined it would be a simple matter of asking them how they had achieved immortality so that he, too, could become one of their number.

Opposite:
The sound of water
cascading down this
many-stepped
waterfall at the
Japanese Garden of
Portland, Oregon, US,
is both exciting and
revitalising.

Towards the end of the Chinese Han period (206 BC–AD 220), a school of Buddhism with a similar theme arose in China, and was later readily accepted in Japan. According to Pure Land Buddhism the Buddha Amida, or Amitabha in China – the Lord of Light – lives in the West in a paradise garden known as the Western Pure Land. There, the trees are laden with jewels like those on the Mystic Isles. Amida takes pity on people who find it hard to achieve enlightenment and declares that anyone who calls on his name will be able to enter the Western Pure Land. Before long, Pure Land Buddhism acquired a huge following, and the popularity of this version inspired Japanese garden designers to develop the Immortal Isles concept further to include Amida. A rocky island was a reminder that immortality could be achieved and the endless cycle of rebirth be broken by calling on Amida. The concept of Amida's Western Paradise was a powerful inspiration to Japanese artists to create some of their most beautiful works in scroll painting, screens and on china.

Buddhism originated in the foothills of the Himalayan Mountains, where, according to legend, the tallest mountain held up the sky. Mount Sumeru, or Meru, reputedly had many similarities with the Mystic Isles. It was marvellously covered in lush trees and shrubs, and the birds and animals had jewel-like qualities. This fable is known as Nine Mountains and Eight Seas, and is represented in some Zen gardens as a visual reminder of the power of the universe.

Rocks were accorded special respect in Shintōism, and were endowed with various qualities. A particularly majestic rock would become a centre for contemplation and the surrounding area was covered with white stones to denote that it was a religious or spiritual place. Rocks became so interwoven with thoughts of attaining spiritual heights that it was entirely natural to incorporate them into the design of a garden, no matter how large or small.

At Daisen'in, in the northern premises of the temple complex of Daitokuji, which was built in 1513 by a Zen priest called Kogaku Soko, there is a group of rocks, or *tsurujima*, representing a crane. The rocks are in the middle of a dry stone river and form part of a larger rock landscape, meant to be viewed as a three-dimensional Chinese painting, from which its composition is derived.

At the Moss Temple of Saihōji, which was developed in the Kamakura period by Musō Sōseki, there is a hall dedicated to Amida. South of the hall is a Jōdo or Pure Land sect pond with islands of white sand symbolizing the Pure Land islands in a misty sea.

Rocks as a basic element

The number three is considered auspicious by Buddhists and represents heaven, earth and humanity. A vertical rock is used to symbolize heaven as the strata of the rock point heavenwards; a rock placed with its breaklines pointing

Opposite:
The romance of a
Japanese garden has
been created by
training an ancient
Wisteria to smother
the roof of this red
lacquered tea house at

Compton Acres,
Dorset. Its twisted
stem adds dignity while
unadorned stepping
stones create a feeling
of naturalness in
keeping with the spirit
of a Zen garden.

Each group of rocks has been designed to be perfectly balanced on its own, or within the group. One could say that rocks placed in a sea of sand also symbolize how each thought within a person's mind or heart should be balanced – once a thought becomes unbalanced, all others are thrown out of kilter. Buddhists aspire to 'no-mind', that is, a mind empty of the fixed categories and conditioned reactions of the limited mind. This 'emptiness' is represented by the sand.

horizontally symbolizes earth; and a diagonally placed rock represents humanity. The temple Tōkai-an takes its name from an area in China where there were said to be three islands or mountains inhabited by Buddhist or Taoist religious men. Three rocks also symbolize the Buddhist trinity – *Sanzon-ishi-gumi* – and are often found in Zen gardens.

The numbers seven and five are also regarded as auspicious by Japanese garden masters, and rocks in Zen gardens are arranged with this in mind. Ryōanji is famous for its composition of 15 rocks in a 7:5:3 layout. These are judiciously positioned in an expanse of white sand that is meticulously raked.

The rocks at Ryōanji are said to represent one of two versions of a Buddhist fable about a tigress and her cubs. It has been copied at the Japanese garden in Portland, Oregon, US, where eight rocks symbolize a tigress who tested the courage of her seven cubs by making them swim across a river. A Buddha nearby feared for their safety and sacrificed himself in the waters in order to save them. The second version of the fable relates how Prince Mahasattva was hunting in the mountains when he found a starving tigress and her cubs. Filled with compassion, he removed his clothes before flinging himself in front of the tigress to provide sustenance for her and her cubs, a noble act ensuring that the Prince would become a Buddha. Both these fables were extremely popular and were widely depicted on scrolls and vases throughout Japan.

Rocks were also used to represent a dragon fable that had its roots in China. Dragon mythology in China and Japan was complex and varied, developing over many centuries. A dragon was a composite of several different animals, and a mixture of Yin and Yang (negative and positive), as it was believed to be both a destroyer and a preserver. The Japanese dragon was able to change shape, but whatever its form it was revered as the Rain Lord and Thunder God. There were five different-coloured dragons, each with different powers. Ultimately, dragons symbolized divine power and, by association, the power of the Emperor, who was considered a divine being. It was even rumoured that one Emperor had a dragon's tail. Dragon gods were thought to have hatched from particularly beautiful stones, which is another reason why they were revered by the Japanese.

At Rokuonji, the temple of the Golden Pavilion (see p. 11), there is a magnificent arrangement of stones representing the story of a carp that became a dragon. The stones are arranged as a waterfall, known as the dragon gate, or *ryūmon*. According to legend, a carp once scaled the waterfall, became a dragon and was then able to fly to heaven. This story could be interpreted as a reminder to those striving for holiness that following a spiritual path is not easy. Courage and perseverance are needed to fight against the main stream of life but the reward for steadfastly keeping to one's spiritual path is enlightenment.

The holiest shrine in Japan is that of the Sun Goddess at Ise-Yatsuhashi, and in temple gardens a rock arranged as an island, with irises on the foreshore, can be read as symbolic of the Tale of Ise. Ise-Yatsuhashi is on the eastern coast of Japan, where a heavenly princess found the lord of garden-making, Sono Tsukuru Kami. She decided this meant the area was a suitable place for a shrine to the sun goddess, and ever since then a shrine has stood close to Sono Tsukuru Kami's garden. By symbolically replicating Ise elsewhere, the sun goddess is brought closer to a greater number of people.

Rocks are endowed with intangible elements that have a strong appeal to the Japanese people. Their texture and size can convey many different elements to those with an open mind. Smooth, low, rounded rocks imbue the surrounding area with a feeling of quiet and gentleness; they have a calm spirit that settles the agitated mind. In contrast, a perpendicular stone that is rough and dark with jagged planes has a dynamic energy that rouses the sleepy soul. A group of high-energy rocks can be almost overwhelming and are usually counterbalanced with a judicious selection of plants nearby.

In dry water gardens, or *karesansui*, the space between rocks is as important as the rocks themselves, and their creation is given very careful thought. *Karesansui* resemble abstract paintings where empty space has an energy of its own. This is most easily understood if you think of a black-and-white photographic negative, where what was solid matter has been reversed but still retains its importance.

Chinese-style painting was somewhat abstract and greatly admired by the Japanese. During the Kamakura period, shoguns collected Chinese paintings. These were to have a profound effect on the design of gardens, which began to develop into a more static and abstract style.

Japanese monks often spent long periods in China learning painting techniques, which they then took back to Japan. Shōhukuji monastery was built in 1382 in the Muromachi period and it is believed that the original garden was of the *karesansui* type, developed from Chinese-style paintings. The Zen monks were renowned for their painting skills and were commissioned to decorate the shogun Yoshimitsu's house. Because Japanese houses had sliding screen walls, it was possible to decorate a screen or hanging scroll with a mountain-and-garden scene, and then to mirror the painting in the garden immediately outside. From this period onwards, Zen-related works of art filtered out from monasteries into the homes of the wealthy.

Opposite:
Emerald green moss lushly carpets the sides of a narrow stream as it gently meanders amongst tall dark trees.

Shōhukuji has a *karesansui* garden built in 1843, with a dry pond, or *kareike*, of white sand and stone that should be viewed from a nearby hall. It is also well known for its *karetaki*, or dry waterfall, and *sanzon* stone grouping. The waterfall is composed of different-shaped rocks and shrubs clipped into mounds. The rocks at the base are smaller and smoother than those at the summit, which are jagged and thrust upwards, implying that the water flows between them rather than over. The smooth stones around the base of the fall suggest calmer waters that gently smooth the rocks into ever-softer shapes. A flat stone bridge positioned towards the summit adds a horizontal dimension, emphasizing the verticals of the mountain rocks. The bridge also reinforces the impression of water tumbling over the rocks. A dry stream in the western section of the garden has its riverbed covered in small, flat, blue-black stones symbolizing the depth and character of the water.

Symbolic sand and gravel

At Myōzenji, Ryōanji and the Japanese Garden in Portland, as well as many other gardens, sand or stone chippings have been used to symbolize space, the sky or the ocean, and also the desired Zen state of 'no-mind' (see p. 21).

Usually the sand or gravel, symbolizing the empty mind, is raked into swirls resembling the way water eddies around stones and islands. The swirls can impart a feeling of raging water or gentle lapping water, depending on their design. Widely spaced ridges imply calmer, flowing water.

Worn and weathered stones and rocks are greatly prized by the Japanese. In some ways this is to do with the great and profound respect they have for their ancestors and for articles with a historical past. Tradition and continuity are fully appreciated, and great care is taken to preserve and maintain symbolic shrines and gardens as they were first conceived: a stone covered with lichen and moss is far more venerated than one that has been newly cut.

This love of stones and rocks is evident at the Como Ordway Memorial Japanese Garden, Minnesota, US, where most of the stones used are between one and four billion years old and have a great geological as well as spiritual significance. They symbolize time in its longest imaginable extent, and therefore the impermanence of all things.

Plants and their symbolism

No garden is complete without at least one plant. Indeed, plants have always played an important part in the lives of the Japanese. Japan is rich in plant life and many of its trees and shrubs have found their way to the West, where they have become so much part of the garden world that many people fail to realize their origins.

One of the most venerated trees is the pine. It is especially loved for its bark, which sometimes resembles the scales of the dragon, and because it symbolizes longevity. It was one of the three trees that grew on the island of P'eng-lai. The pine, plum and peach were known as the Trees of Life. In China, there had even been a pine-tree cult, whose members believed that infusions of pine needles, cones or sap had the power to prolong life, provided the decoction was taken regularly. The Chinese and the Japanese

A simple wooden zigzag walkway designed to confound bad spirits hugs a joyful planting of Japanese Iris.

believed it was significant that pine trees were evergreen. They thought that a 3,000-year-old pine had resin or sap in the shape of dragons, and if it was consumed in large-enough quantities, the partaker would live for 500 years.

A pine contorted by the wind evokes powerful images of storms sweeping down from majestic mountains, of driving rain blowing and buffeting the tree into a fantastic shape. It is a tree that overcomes all difficulties, and is symbolic of human life triumphing over adversity.

During the Heian period (794–1185), Sei Shonagon, a court lady who served the Empress, often noted in her pillow book (an oblong box used as a headrest at night) the importance of different plants, shrubs and trees. This was an era when every courtly person had to develop the art of composing short poems suited to various occasions. More often than not, a flower or tree would be referred to in order to imply an unspoken thought.

Red pines were believed to have a strong female presence, or Yin, which would counterbalance an area that might be strongly Yang, or male. In Chinese paintings, pines are usually depicted in a stylized form. This is because Chinese painting developed in such a way that different emotions were conveyed to the viewer through different brushstrokes. Interestingly, one of the best inks for painting was made from pine soot.

Chinese landscape painting had a powerful effect on Japanese garden design. In the Edo period, gardens became more stylized and pine trees were pruned to replicate the trees of Chinese scroll paintings. Japanese painters did develop their own style of painting, though rather less formal, this, too, affected the design of gardens.

Scroll-style gardens have come to epitomize Japanese gardens for some westerners who have not had the opportunity to visit one of the many authentic Japanese gardens in the West. At the Japanese Garden in Portland, Oregon, US, and at Compton Acres in Dorset, England, there are pine trees in a less formal setting, cleverly pruned to give them an ageless quality that is calming and serene.

The plum tree is one of Japan's favourite trees. The Japanese have a lunar calendar, with plum blossom appearing in the first lunar month and cherry trees in the second. Plum blossom symbolized the beginning of the New Year and its beauty was thought to be enhanced by a light covering of snow. Because it evidently survived the winter it was thought of as a strong plant and came to represent the quiet strength of a true man. In Heian times, a noble might present a pretty lady with a poem and a branch of plum

Opposite:
Attractive authentic
stone lanterns placed
at strategic points add
a reflective element
that is purely Zen in
character.

camellia came to symbolize that in the midst of life there is death.

The bamboo was another revered plant; the bamboo, the pine and the plum were looked on as the Three Friends of Winter. The bamboo was associated with the moon, and the moon with the dragon. One fable recounts how a holy man cut down a bamboo so that it would turn into a dragon, which then carried him to the moon; why he wanted to go to the moon, no one knows.

blossom, denoting that it came from a respectable and worthy man.

The Japanese people's deep love of nature led them to look forward to the progress of the seasons. Sei Shonagon also made constant references in her pillow book to the weather and the expectation of a certain plant being in leaf or flower at a certain time, even on a particular day. Although Zen gardens have few perennial plants growing in them, there are usually shrubs or trees that act as pointers for the time of year. Zen temples grew the native red-flowering camellia, which was not planted in private gardens because its flowers tended to fall in mid-bloom. However, Zen priests used this characteristic to demonstrate that man can be in the first flush of life, yet death can still find him out. So the

The Japanese loved the qualities of the moon. They appreciated how its silver light made a landscape seem mysterious and romantic, and admired the way plum and cherry blossom gently glowed in its soft light. In the Chinese pond-style gardens of the Heian period, courtiers enjoyed moonlit boating trips. Indeed, a landscape is transformed when seen by a clear moon. In our modern world, street lights obscure the night sky and we are rarely able to appreciate the magnificence of a starry sky and full moon. A sheet of water, however small or large, reflects the sky. Boating on a starry night would have been a magical experience, with the ink-black sky alight with a myriad of twinkling stars. The reflection of the sky in the water would give the boaters the impression that they were sailing in space, between two skies. The wind rustling in the large thickets of bamboo would reinforce the feeling of sailing on a vast ocean in a sea breeze.

Acers are associated in most people's minds with Japanese gardens. Many have beautifully coloured leaves in spring and autumn, and they are primarily grown to emphasize the fresh spirit of spring and the richness of the shortening autumn days. Since much of Japan has moist summer months, any plant that becomes more attractive when wet is greatly prized. The leaves of Acer palmatum vary according to the variety but many are finely cut and lace-like. When covered with dew or rain, they become even more beautiful; sunlight catches the trillions of droplets, making the branches appear smothered in masses of jewels, like the trees on the Mystic Isles (see p. 16).

Because of the damp climate, moss is a natural groundcover for the temple gardens in Kyōto. The Moss Garden of Saihōji has more than 40 different mosses that express the richness of life. Moss has the qualities of quietness and calm – the *karesansui* garden east of the study have been trimmed and trained to resemble a treasure ship that travelled to the jewel-covered Hōraito islands. Behind the ship, more bushes have been pruned to resemble the ocean waves. Here, too, is a mystical turtle shaped from a bush. In some gardens, azaleas are allowed to flower, and because they are severely pruned they do so profusely, appearing as floating pink or white clouds. Allowing them to flower is linked with the desire to emphasize the time of year.

essence of Zen gardens. Moss covering the ground in a temple garden also demonstrates the attitude of 'going with the flow'. If grass cannot grow in a situation but moss thrives, then it is moss that wins the day. Grass swaying in the breeze conveys a feeling of movement and action, while the stillness of moss grounds one's thoughts. The brilliance of moss is sometimes emphasized by a subtle planting alongside of the Chinese bell flower, *Platyerium grandiflorum*, which is usually a rich blue in colour.

The small-leaved azalea is often used in Zen gardens because it tolerates hard pruning, making it suitable for shaping into mounds resembling clouds. At Jikoin, by the *hōjō*, there is a *karesansui* garden representing mountain scenery, where large azalea bushes are clipped into solid, smooth mounds to give the feeling of permanence, at the same time symbolizing a mountain range. At Daichiji, azalea bushes in the

A group of shrubs planted in a garden can symbolize a wood. Such shrubs are pruned to resemble the gentle outline of a clump of trees when seen from a distance. In essence they are like groups of shrubs or trees depicted in screen or scroll ink paintings. Often shrubs of this kind would be used in a 'borrowed scenery', or *shakkei* garden. These were popular in Zen temples in the Muromachi period and later, when gardens became smaller and there was a need to link the garden with the landscape beyond its perimeters. Incorporating the distant scenery into the design of the garden was popular with Buddhist priests as it was one way to demonstrate that each object in the world was part of the whole. Priests would select 10 landmarks linked to the temple and its garden. At Shōden-ji in Kyōto, the guardian mountain of Kyōto is incorporated into the garden design by allowing a distant view of it to be glimpsed through tall trees immediately outside the garden. This creates three planes – a distant, middle and foreground – bringing depth and harmony to the garden.

The lotus flower was revered because it grew in water and was therefore intimately connected with the source of life. One of the most important sutras (discourses of the Buddha or of a great teacher) is the Lotus sutra, in which it is said that one who lives and learns by Yakuo Bosatsu's teaching will be reborn on a lotus flower in Amida's Pure Land. Buddhists equate the lotus, which grows out of the muddy depths of a pond, with the idea of beauty and purity growing out of darkness and impurity.

Water – the vital element

Without water there can be no life, and therefore it was natural that Shintō, which revered nature, should attach enormous importance to the role of water in the life of mankind. In China and Japan, there were stories of the miraculous water of life. The Chinese Emperor Wu Ti, who died in 87 BC, was said to have built a tall tower, on top of which was placed a jug. This was designed to catch the life-prolonging dew believed to fall from the stars at night.

At Ryōgen, the area in front of the *hōjō* is raked into long, even ridges, which are interrupted by two smooth mounds of sand. The general impression is of a vast ocean that stretches serenely into the distance. A brilliant addition was made to the garden in 1958 by developing a small area, or *tsuboniwa*, north of the *hōjō*, into a dry water garden quite different from the large one. Around a small, flat rock the sand has been raked into expanding circles, symbolizing busy, eddying water, or how one's thoughts ripple outwards.

All Japanese gardens have either actual water in the form of a pond or a lake, or a dry stone water garden (*karesansui*). Great care was taken when designing water features so that they were of the right character for the surrounding area. At Kenchōji, the garden is designed on the theme of Mount Hōrai, or Mountains of the Blest (see p. 16). Shrubs clipped into gentle mounds impart a tranquil character to the pond-viewing area. The water here is smooth and calm, reflecting the surrounding greenery. Eihōji has a contrasting pond, belonging to the 'stroll-around' style garden. The pond covers a larger expanse than at Kenchōji, so that it mirrors not only the surrounding landscape but also the sky, and the energy of the pond is made greater here than at Kenchōji by the introduction of a waterfall flowing down a steep rocky projection.

In dry stone gardens, sand is raked to imitate the energy of real water.

Water is an intricate part of a tea garden or *roji*. At Shintō shrines, there was often a source of water where worshippers rinsed their hands to symbolize the purification of their souls. Sei Shonagon wrote that Shintō purification services could be performed by a Buddhist priest or by a practitioner of Yin-Yang, who was known as a Master of Divination. In tea gardens, water has a similar role. It is customary to position a source of water near the entrance to the tea house so that the mouth can be rinsed before the ceremony begins. A Yin-Yang custom was that water should flow from east to west, which it does in most Zen gardens.

Architectural elements and their importance

Various architectural features imbue a Japanese garden with its intangible characteristics. A subdued taste, *wabi*, ensures a timeless feel to a garden, which the Japanese have always appreciated. The earliest holy men lived in simple huts of earth and thatch that were in harmony with the surrounding countryside. Tea houses derive their characteristics from these early buildings. Small, subtle differences might be deployed in their construction, which would be of significance only to those with a trained eye; the grain of the wood used said much about the owner to the educated of the time. In the Edo period, when refinement meant everything, even slight variations in a particular object or the way in which it was used could be full of unspoken meaning.

Japanese gardens are renowned for their lanterns, which became an intricate part of the tea garden. Just as ancient rocks were coveted by the owners of new gardens and often taken from old gardens that had fallen into disrepair, so lanterns aged with lichen and moss were greatly sought after. Their quiet character added substance and gravitas to what was usually a small, enclosed area. They were,

Below:
In a quiet corner of the Japanese Garden at Golden Gate Park, San Francisco, a miniature, snow topped Mount Fuji has been created to remind Japanese people of their most loved mountain.

and still are, a visual reminder that the *roji* should be approached with the right frame of mind – reflective and contemplative.

Pagodas are often seen in Japanese gardens, including the Golden Gate Park in San Francisco, the Japanese garden in Portland, Oregon, US, at Eihōji and at Erinji. Although the pagodas are of different sizes and forms, they all bear a wealth of Buddhist symbolism, having developed into this complex and elegant form out of simple Indian burial mounds, called *stupas*. Pagodas humanize a garden; they also help in the manipulation of scale within it. Where shrubs symbolize trees and mountains, a small, weathered pagoda can reinforce the illusion that one is looking at a larger landscape.

Sensory elements

For the Japanese, one of the most important elements of a Japanese garden is its quietness but, unfortunately, many

Opposite:
**Tucked protectively
amongst dark pines
and scarlet acers this
noble building stands
sentinel above Kyōto.**

Too much sun can make a pond seem hard and inhospitable, whereas a pond with shrubs and rocks positioned by it, casting shadows and reflections, becomes gentle and inviting. Feather-pruned acers allow light to filter through their canopy so that soft shadows are cast on the moss below. Heavy shadows can be menacing; they block out all the sun, making it difficult for any groundcover to grow well. Conversely, light shadows dance with the breeze, adding yet another dimension to the garden.

are visited in such great numbers that this vital quality is lost. The gardens in Kyōto and at Golden Gate Park attract thousands of visitors who sometimes have little concept of the benefits of looking quietly at a garden. Still, the gardens are well worth visiting at their least busy times, as they still have all the characteristics of a true Japanese garden. The *wabi* atmosphere, which is so much a part of a Zen garden, can be experienced there but fleetingly; it is a fragile quality.

It is clear that creating a garden with a reflective, calm atmosphere is no quick or easy matter. Most Japanese garden masters take time to approach the garden with a peaceful spirit. The way the sun and moon travel around the garden is studied in order that everything, from the smallest plant to the largest rock, may be positioned in the most beneficial way.

Too much light alters the subtle feeling of mystery that pervades a group of trees.

Japanese gardens are mostly green but these greens become varied and exciting when consideration is given to the effect of sunlight. A Japanese garden master skillfully manipulates the available sunlight so that even on a cloudy day the different greens of shrubs, trees and groundcover plants are shown to best advantage. Each item in the garden is positioned with love and respect.

The sensory image a Zen garden makes is one of its most enduring qualities. A garden that appeals to the inner self in an intangible way invites and even compels a person to return. Dappled light soothes the spirit and lowers the stress levels. Sound is also a powerful element. The swishing of bamboo on a hot day speaks of the ocean and transports one into another realm. The gentle gurgle of a stream over pebbles lightens the heart and encourages the child to resurface within the adult. Sparkling waterfalls add a refreshing sound that calls to mind tranquil mountains in distant lands. With these sights and sounds one is able to go

on a mental journey to a place that is unconnected with turmoil, strife, aggression and cruelty. By distancing oneself from the everyday world it is possible to invite harmony and peace back into one's life.

Understanding a little of the beliefs and thoughts of the makers of these gardens makes it easier to adapt appropriate features to a western garden. To achieve the wonderful spirit of a Japanese garden, it is necessary to begin to understand what was, and is, important to the designers, developers and builders. With an indepth knowledge of a style of gardening, superficiality is avoided and a garden that feels well established can be created. Japanese gardens are designed to be complete at their creation, rather than developing piecemeal over a number of years. It is this ability to design them as a complete whole that gives Japanese gardens their steady and stable atmosphere, which is so attractive in this rapidly changing world.

Buddha law,

Shining

In leaf dew.

Issa

WATER

Creating balance and tranquillity

Creating balance The smallest area of water immediately brings a new dimension to a garden. The Japanese and Chinese still acknowledge that water is one of the main life forces in the natural world. Through Shintōism, it came to play a central part in the lives of the Japanese, who revered water for its purifying properties – not only of the body but also of the spirit within.

Water brings a freshness to a garden that is particularly beneficial when the weather is oppressive and sultry. On still, airless days the sound of a waterfall, whatever its size, introduces a lively note to a garden. Indeed, sound invariably triggers an emotional response that is connected to the past. Listening to running water may bring back memories of paddling in a brook when a child, of hot, tired feet experiencing the sudden coolness of water passing through spread toes, or the feel of smooth pebbles viewer to see them with new eyes. Cloud reflections link the garden with the sky above, creating a feeling of distance and space. It is this feeling of space that allows us to relax and shed our worries. Reflections of surrounding shrubs and trees give these plants double the impact that they would otherwise have. The reflection of a noble, ancient pine leaning over a sheet of dark, limpid water affords a new view that can only emphasize the beauty of its blue-green needles and dragon-scale bark.

A pond gives the gardener the opportunity to introduce water-loving plants to a plot. In turn, this bigger selection of plants encourages wildlife to frequent a pond. There is a tremendous thrill in watching dragonflies emerge from their ugly and fearsome nymph state among iris leaves. Watching damselflies and dragonflies dip and dart over even a small pond is so absorbing that day-to-day problems seem to disappear.

Long before agriculture evolved, man had observed the characteristics of water. Primitive man learnt quickly that wherever there was water, there would be plants, fish and animals. Water sources were vital to the well-being and good health of man, as they still are. As he learnt how to harness and manipulate water, agriculture developed.

beneath the soles of the feet while refreshing spring water eddies around tired ankles. The sound of lapping water can bring back memories of crisp, sunlit days when a stiff breeze whips the surface of the river against the side of a moored rowing boat, as birds dip and wheel in a clear blue sky overhead.

Ponds introduce light and life to a garden in a unique way. The smallest can reflect the sky and plants close by; the dark depths of a tiny pond or water bowl hidden among shrubs will manage to reflect back a jewel of light that is all the more valuable in a gloomy area. A larger pond reflects clouds and any surrounding scenery on a grander scale, allowing the

Once the Japanese had learnt how to control water and become successful rice growers, it was natural that these skills should be used in the creation of pleasure gardens. The Japanese and Chinese have long glorified nature within the boundaries of the garden, unlike early Mediterranean, Egyptian and Middle Eastern gardeners, who saw nature as threatening and as a result created well-ordered gardens, surrounded by walls or enclosures to distance the garden owner from the wildness of the world beyond. Within these garden settings, natural elements such as water, plants and stone were tamed into somewhat rigid designs to demonstrate man's power over nature, and ponds were either oblong or square. On the other hand, Japanese ponds were always an irregular shape, as they are in their natural state.

Japan can experience heavy winter snowfalls, which transform ponds and waterfalls into fairy-tale scenes. The visual effect of snow on the landscape has always been popular with the Japanese, and has long been a favourite subject for artists to depict on scroll paintings and china. One of the most renowned is Utagawa Hiroshige, the woodblock-print artist who published *The Fifty-Three Stations of the Tōdaidō Road* in the early 1830s. Many of his prints portray well-known mountains and lakes covered in deep snow. He used a covering of snow to highlight the dark green of pine needles and to define clearly the banks of rivers and streams so that the moving water contrasts with the static snow.

Snow and ice accent the basic design of water features, allowing familiar scenes to be viewed with fresh eyes. A Japanese garden covered in snow becomes more abstract, and unfrozen ponds and streams appear more spatial when surrounded by snow-smothered plants and trees. The purity of snow is greatly loved by the Japanese as another manifestation of the purity of water.

One of the greatest influences on Japanese garden design came from China in AD 607, when news reached the Japanese court of a marvellous garden, the Western Park, belonging to Sui Yan Ti, the Han Emperor. A court official, Ono no Imoko, went to China to see the garden for himself. It was truly impressive, with five lakes and four 'seas'. One of the seas had a shoreline of 24 kilometres (13 miles) and in it were three rocky islands representing

Below:
On a hot sunny day, inky black water reflects the blue sky above and a decorative lantern hidden from view behind a dwarf pine.

Opposite:
Lovingly placed rocks
have been positioned
to create a two-step
waterfall which slows
the water's flow and
orchestrates a
soothing, cooling
sound that revives the
flagging spirit.

the Mystic Isles of the Blest. Each lake was connected to the next by a canal that allowed courtiers to sail in highly decorated pleasure boats from lake to lake. Ono no Imoko returned home so impressed with the Emperor's Western Park that it became the most influential model for Japanese garden design for centuries to come. For the next six to seven hundred years, ponds were usually the central theme of Japanese gardens, with plants and rocks designed around them.

During the Heian period (794–1185), ponds often took on lake-size proportions, and the surrounding scenery was usually designed to be seen from a boat. A pavilion built on the water's edge added a Chinese touch and afforded a site where musicians could play melodious music to the boaters. This created a deeply romantic and relaxing atmosphere, which the Heian courtiers felt was in keeping with their love of nature and poetry. Indeed, it was fashionable to compose short poems while boating.

Large pond-style gardens were designed with paths running through the trees and shrubs so that less privileged people could enjoy the garden on foot. One existing garden from the Muromachi period (1333–1573), but in the Heian style, is Ginkaku-ji, or the Silver Pavilion. From woodcuts of the original design, one can see that it was intended more as a 'stroll-around' garden. Also Heian in style is Lake Biwa near Kyōto. On the left bank there is a small wooden temple built on piers to stand above the water. Known as the Floating Temple, it gives the visitor the impression that the world has been left behind and one is hovering between the cool depths of the lake and the infinite space of the sky.

The lavishly built Golden Pavilion, or Kinkaku-ji, in Kyōto does not hover over the water but is built on a projecting shoreline or island. A covered walkway, or *sosei*, over the water enables visitors to gaze into the dark depths of the lake. The Golden Pavilion was built in 1397 during the Muromachi period by the retired shogun Yoshimitsu as his palace, but he always intended that it should become a Buddhist temple on his death.

The temple of the Golden Pavilion is justly famous for its waterfall, known as the dragon-gate waterfall, or ryūmon. It represents the fable of the carp that became a dragon, a popular myth from China that was the basis for the design of many waterfalls both in Japan and in Japanese gardens in the West (see p. 22). A group of large stones has been positioned together to create a single

waterfall that falls steeply on to a diagonally positioned stone representing a carp. The carp stone breaks the line at the base of the fall, making it appear more naturalistic as the water splashes and bounces off it into the pool. The energy of this water feature is palpable.

Waterfalls are used in Japanese gardens to energize a particular space. An area that might feel too passive could be enlivened with the addition of a multiple fall with a great deal of splashing and gurgling. A single fall would produce a more continuous sound, which would be more restful and more appropriate as background noise.

Waterfalls also add height and interest to a garden, but they are only designed by Japanese garden masters who have made an intensive study of real waterfalls. They observe the way water falls in different ways depending on the height of the fall and the shape of the rocks on to which the water splashes. It was noticed long ago that waterfalls fell either singly or in

Most waterfalls are designed to have their flow of water broken, which is achieved in a number of ways. It can be interrupted at a point between the top and bottom of the rockface. If interrupted once, it is known as a 'two-step' fall; broken twice, it is a 'three-step' fall. Both types can have one of their stages broken by placing a rock in the path of a continuous flow of water to divide it. In this way, a waterfall that starts as a single flowing fall can be divided into as many falls as desired. The more falls that are introduced, the busier the water appears.

a series of falls. The different sound that single and multiple falls make is considered an important element in the general character of the area where a waterfall is positioned.

Catching the sun down its entire length, a single fall could appear like a silver ribbon linking the rocky heights with the dark, cool waters below. Or it could be designed to create a continuous curtain of falling water. This was engineered by removing any stones or rocks from the path of the water, and, if possible, the beginning of the fall would project slightly out from the rockface. A single fall could be given a different character by placing rocks at strategic intervals at its mouth; this is known as a 'thread fall' because it is divided into different strands that all run smoothly to the water below.

The carp stones (see p. 18) at the foot of the waterfall at the Golden Pavilion, and at the Japanese Garden in Portland, Oregon, US, act as a water-divider. The effect is particularly attractive as the water has been designed to fall in a continuous sheet from above. It hits the carp stone with such force that it produces a shower of sparkling droplets that make a refreshing pattering noise. At Como Ordway Memorial Japanese garden in the US, the thread fall is broken by several rocks placed on a ledge just above the level of the pond. This has created an intensity of splashing water above the smoothness of the pool below. In contrast, in the Japanese garden at Golden Gate Park, San Francisco, the waterfall travels discreetly over a rockface planted with many shrubs. This results in glimpses of the waterfall snatched here and there, and the whole effect is one of naturalness and mystery.

Some waterfalls are artfully designed so that the water flows from left to right or right to left. Greater interest can be created by dividing a left- or right-hand fall at some point down the rockface so that it changes direction, to fall in a zigzag pattern. In the Japanese garden in Portland, there is just such a short waterfall, or cascade, between two ponds. It adds an energetic note between two tranquil points that is unexpected, bringing the mind sharply into focus.

Islands

Islands composed of a single rock or a collection of rocks were placed in Japanese ponds to add interest to that particular area or to remind the viewer of an important religious myth. A large pond was felt to be more naturalistic with the inclusion of one or more islands. The size of the island had to balance the size of the pond to make it more believable. Very large ponds, or lakes, covering several

The fluid mirrored
surface of this stream
is balanced by a
walkway of solid
stepping stones set
amongst graceful
bulrushes that sway
in the breeze.

acres could easily accommodate substantial islands, which might replicate the magical three islands of Hōraito that lie somewhere in the West, in mythology. In temple gardens, ponds or lakes were not usually built on such an unwieldy scale, so Buddhist garden masters designed rocky islands relating to the myth of the Isles of the Blest and, by extension, to Amida's Pure Land (see pp. 16–18).

Many temple ponds were designed to be viewed from one of the temple buildings. Islands built in this type of pond give the garden a strong focal point, helping to anchor the garden and give it substance, so that it is always a pleasure to view. The island could be composed of one carefully placed rock so that the impact of its character might be greater. Or it could be constructed of a number of rocks placed in a ring and infilled with earth to support a planting of trees, shrubs and grass.

At the Golden Pavilion, the 'stroll-around' garden pond has several islands in front of the pavilion, which lie low in the water. The ancient pines growing on them have been pruned to replicate the shape of pines in Chinese scroll paintings, which were so admired when the garden was first laid out. They are kept to a size that corresponds in a harmonious and balanced way to the depth and breadth of the islands on which they are growing. At Tatton Park in Cheshire, England, there is a small, hundred-year-old Japanese garden with an island whose planting has been kept in keeping with the island's size by regular pruning. Again, this type of verdant island could represent the Mystic Isles of the Blest or Amida's Pure Land, since both were said to be lushly planted with shrubs and trees.

However, some pond designers preferred the more abstract imagery of a sea turtle or crane island. Turtle islands are usually composed of a headstone (often the largest and most powerful stone of the group, positioned to imply that the turtle is looking

in a particular direction), and leg and tail stones that are often of different sizes but usually placed flat side uppermost. Sometimes the turtle will have an additional rock on its back to symbolize a baby turtle. A good example can be seen at Ikōji, where the turtle island is quite large and has been used to give perspective to that particular part of the garden.

At Old Shūrinji garden, which is in the grounds of the Koshōji temple, there is a splendid example of a turtle or *kamejima* island group, and close by is an upright rock symbolizing the mountain Horaizan (see p. 64). The turtle island is composed of various rocks of different shapes and sizes. The flat side of each rock has been placed uppermost to indicate the hard, flat smoothness of the sea turtle's skin. A large rock has been placed at one end, pointing upwards but on a slight diagonal, with the rough strata of the rock impling that this is the turtle's head looking upwards. The central area between the rocks has been filled with soil and planted with low-growing grass; this represents the turtle's shell, emphasizing its legs and head. By using an upright rock for the head in contrast to the flatter stones representing the turtle's legs, a certain liveliness has been introduced to the creation.

Crane islands are more abstract than turtle islands, and of a simpler construction. The largest stone often represents the crane's outstretched wings, while a thin, low line of smaller rocks may symbolize its head and neck. This type of arrangement is known as *tsurujima*, and can be used to add visual depth and character to an area of pond.

Another abstract arrangement of rocks might represent the Three Buddha rocks or *sanzon*. Three rocks of varying shapes and sizes are positioned close to each other but with great regard to the spaces created between them. This is carried out in much the same way as an artist places his or her brush on a piece of paper; the brushstroke can be much more powerful when it is placed with consideration to the space around it. Therefore, a well-positioned

group of rocks brings a pond to life and animates it in a subtle but powerful way.

The shoreline of a pond is very important in a Japanese garden. It is the shoreline that helps to define the shape of the pond or stream. It can be strong and dynamic or gentle and subdued; it can create a strong defining line between the water and the surrounding garden, or it can gently bring the water and land together so that one is hardly aware where one begins and the other ends.

At the famous Moss Garden of Saihōji, the banks of the pond and island are subdued and gentle. Originally, this was designed as a Jōdo, or Pure Land, garden (see p. 18), in the early Kamakura period, but over the intervening years more than 40 different mosses have been allowed to clothe the ground beneath the tall trees. The banks of the pond and island are composed of different-sized rocks, to give the impression that the banks are slowly collapsing. These rocks are now covered with mosses, so that the bank appears to extend right down to the water. The feeling is of extreme tranquillity and mystery. Here, too, there are islands composed of white sand, suggesting islands seen through a veil of mist across a wide ocean. This idea was developed to a fine degree in dry sand gardens.

The pond garden of Fumon'in in the grounds of Tōfukuji is small and open, the opposite of the Moss Garden. It is close to the Founder's Hall, or Kaizando, so it is not at all private or mysterious. A long walkway runs its entire length. Between

the hard, straight edge of the path and the narrow pond is a textural arrangement of rocks and low shrubs clipped into mounds. The smooth, green mounds of shrubs echo the rounded shapes of the water-lily pads that cover the pond surface, giving the impression that the pond is larger than it really is. Clipped shrubs are placed among the surrounding rocks. The theme of clipped shrubs has been carried through to the hillside behind the pond, and also to the other side of the path. By threading a single design feature from one area to another, a sense of balance and harmony has been created.

At Tentoku-in temple, Japanese irises have been used to hide the edges of the pond and to link one area with another. The irises do not line the entire pond edge but are judiciously planted in blocks interspersed with grass that almost reaches the water's surface. There is an island in the pond where moss- and lichen-covered rocks project out among another planting of tall, straight irises.

The smoothness of their leaves echoes the smoothness of the water and highlights the solidity of the rocks.

At Taizō-in, a three-tiered waterfall flows down into a pond enclosed by large rocks. The last flow of the waterfall before it finally meets the pond is over smooth, flattish pebbles. This gives the impression of a mountain waterfall and stream. Each pebble has been carefully positioned so that the water flows in a highly naturalistic manner, eddying here and there on its way to the last low fall.

Smooth pebbles tell of hundreds of years of being washed continuously by cool mountain streams. They are all the more beautiful when washed by the rain, when their subtle blues, greys, greens and browns come alive. At the Missouri Botanical Garden in the US, blue-grey flat pebbles have been used to edge part of the four-acre (1.6 hectare) lake. Here, the bank slopes gently into the water and the pebbles have been used to create a mountain shingle beach that is all the more attractive in the rain. In contrast, another area of the lake has been edged with wooden logs. These tend to impart an unnatural quality to the area because they are of a uniform size and shape, which is less in keeping with an authentic Japanese garden where the aim is always to replicate the asymmetrical character of nature.

At the Fort Worth Botanic Garden Center in Texas, US, dynamic brown and blue rocks create a curtain waterfall. Some distance from the fall, smaller rocks have been placed flat side uppermost to project into the pond. At points where the rocks link the bank with the water, pebbles form small 'beaches', like those found beside surging torrents of water in mountainous areas of the world.

Bridges

Bridges play an important part in the design of a Japanese garden and should harmonize with their surroundings, bringing a positive element to the garden. Sometimes they play a symbolic role, representing mankind's journey from earth to a spiritual paradise. There are a great many different bridge designs, each emphasizing the particular character of the area of the garden where the bridge has been built.

An ancient Chinese belief associated with Feng Shui, or geomancy, was that evil travelled in straight lines. Bridges designed on a zigzag pattern were thus deemed to confound the evil spirits, who were unable to negotiate corners and so fell into the water. Feng Shui also holds that uninterrupted straight lines are a good conductor of evil forces. To mitigate the bad Feng Shui of a straight bridge, careful thought was given to the planting at each end of it, and to how its design merged with the supporting banks. A flat-stone bridge would therefore be positioned between rocks that were slightly upthrusting at each end. Another ploy to deflect the bad Feng Shui was to place the bridge at an angle over the water. At the same time this helped to bring a naturalistic element to the area.

Large Chinese gardens traditionally had brightly painted or lacquered bridges. These introduced a light-hearted feeling to the garden, in keeping with its role as somewhere to relax in and compose poems. As Japanese Zen gardens were designed to calm the mind as a prerequisite for enlightenment, highly coloured bridges were obviously inappropriate. Instead, Zen garden masters favoured natural materials such as stone, wood and turf.

Early Japanese gardens sometimes had a single-stone slab bridge to link a part of a garden to an island. Such bridges were valued for their dynamic energy. The size and weight imbued the stone with an intangible power that the Japanese deeply respected. More commonly, though, a stone slab bridge would have been made of two or more spans, owing to the difficulty of obtaining and placing very long stones. This allowed the bridge to be designed slightly off-balance, which was more in keeping with the natural world.

At Reitōin garden, which is within the ancient garden of Japan's largest Zen temple, there is a pond with a three-stone span bridge – the oblong chiselled stones

create a feeling of quiet strength while emphasizing the calm smoothness of the water. The powerful horizontal lines of the bridge emphasize the large perpendicular stone behind it and the naturalistic planting on the far side of the pond. The pond is viewed from the abbot's drawing room and may act as a reminder that when making a spiritual journey the traveller should not be deflected from his or her path by worldly distractions, but must concentrate on keeping to his or her chosen path.

At Old Shūrinji, the pond has a single-slab stone bridge that sits discreetly among surrounding rocks. The pond is famous for its curved banks that are lined with weighty rocks, and the smooth, straight lines of the bridge add balance and perspective in a way that a curved bridge could not achieve. The garden of Chikurin'in is justly famous for its blue slab bridges that link islands among gentle mounds of azalea and pines pruned into cloud shapes.

The idea of using a bridge to contrast with the surrounding garden has been used at the Mankōji garden. This was built in the Edo period, around 1766, and has a steep hillside covered with much-admired stone groupings. At the foot of the powerful upright rocks there is a pond, spanned by a rustic bridge constructed of tree trunks covered with earth and grass. The curved expanse of grass makes a pleasing contrast with the roughness of the rocks, while a turf bridge enlivens this part of the garden in a harmonious way.

This type of Japanese bridge has been copied in many western Japanese gardens and is similar to the one at Eihōji, which is a 'stroll-around' Heian-style garden, so that the bridge had to be suitable for walking on in a leisurely way. Known as a *Musaikyō* bridge, it is constructed of wood and gently arches over the large expanse of water. Supported on wooden piles, it has a curved wooden handrail, interrupted in the middle by a porch, or decorative roof. The overall impression is one of grace and elegance, which, at the same time, encourages the walker to slow his or her pace and enjoy the garden in a leisurely manner.

A similar bridge, but without the centrally placed porch, can be seen at the Missouri Botanical Garden. Known as the Drum Bridge, it adds an air of elegance to this part of the garden and looks very beautiful in winter when nearby trees appear as black silhouettes under a blanket of pure white snow against a blue-grey sky. (There is also a zigzag bridge and azalea bushes are clustered

around each end of it, symbolizing the beginning and the end of a journey over water.) Drum bridges originated in China and were so shaped to allow for the passage of junks. At Compton Acres in Dorset, England, there is a miniature drum bridge lacquered a vibrant scarlet. The Japanese tea house has been painted the same colour, and in autumn it also flames in the various acers, introducing a Chinese flavour to the garden.

A flat wooden-board bridge made of unpainted wood so that the natural grain can be appreciated and admired is very much in the Zen style. Laid simply across a stream, it evokes *wabi*, a subdued rustic atmosphere, in the garden. In many gardens open to the public, however, this type of bridge has been replaced with a more serviceable structure – one that does not absorb the wet and become slippery underfoot.

In Golden Gate Park in San Francisco, there is a highly textural bridge that meets various Zen design requirements. Strictly

speaking, it is not a bridge because it is composed of a number of deep, shaped rocks set into the water. The flat-topped rocks have been placed at random intervals, but are close enough together to allow people to cross the water. The gaps between the stones require walkers to think of where they are placing their feet, and by concentrating on this act other niggling problems are briefly laid to one side. This is a good Zen ploy to help its students loosen their hold on everyday concerns and empty their minds.

Making a pond and waterfall

Creating a water feature is just one way of bringing the paradise world of the Immortals into the world that we inhabit. With such a feature it is possible to go on an emotional journey far away from everyday cares. The sound of running water soothes the soul and aids contemplation and relaxation.

A pond should never be made on impulse. Great thought and consideration should be given to its placement, shape and construction material. Although a pond can be one of the most expensive outlays in a garden, it can also be deeply rewarding. As it is one of the most permanent features in a plot, it does need to be designed correctly from the outset. Having to rectify any faults at a later stage can prove time-consuming, difficult and expensive.

For the best results, a pond, waterfall or stream should be planned before any other feature within the garden. Ponds are the central theme in many Japanese gardens and have been since the Heian period (794–1185 AD). The position of a pond depends on the location of the garden. In northern European countries and the far north of North America and Canada, intense summer heat is not usually a problem, and ponds and streams can withstand fairly open conditions, although they should not be in full sunlight for more than four to six

hours a day. However, any site likely to heat up a great deal during the day should be avoided. This is because the more the water temperature fluctuates, the harder it is to keep the water clear and 'sweet'. Ideally, the water temperature of a pond should change little between noon and midnight, and the more stable the temperature, the better.

Choose a site that is not overhung by trees, because leaves falling into the water will build up at the bottom of the pond and alter the oxygen levels. The way light falls on a water feature can enhance its beauty. Dappled shadows help to create an air of tranquillity and mystery, as at the Moss Garden, while buildings and rock groupings cast solid shadows, which can be an attractive addition to the character of the pond.

Having chosen the best site for a water feature, consideration must be given to how the pond will function. Will it contain fish or simply be a home for frogs and dragonflies? If it is to be stocked with fish,

Opposite:
A series of shallow
waterfalls allows water
to slowly and gently
make its way past
tall Gunnera and
a profusion of Lady's
Mantle.

it should be at least one metre (nearly 3 feet) deep. Many pre-formed ponds are relatively shallow, roughly half a metre (nearly 2 feet) deep. A pond of this depth will heat up faster than one twice that depth, and in hot weather fish will lack oxygen and become distressed. There is also more likelihood of the pond growing unsightly algae blooms, which, once established, are hard to eradicate.

Specialist pond suppliers stock everything one needs to create a pond. They will usually provide measurements to follow when digging the water feature, so that the water surface is of the correct ratio to the depth. A pond with the right surface/depth ratio will be trouble-free year after year, so it is well worth getting right.

Thick pond-lining material is by far the best material to use. Concrete can pose endless problems if it cracks in a severe winter or very hot summer. Pond liners are ideal when designing a Japanese pond, which should be of an irregular shape, as

they fold into the different contours. Liners are usually guaranteed for 20 years and, should they be punctured at some stage, can be repaired in a similar way to a bicycle tyre.

Once the function of the pond has been decided, next comes the positioning of the waterfall, if there is to be one. Mark out where the pond will be dug with a line or sticks. Step back and decide on three points in the garden from which the pond will be seen. The point at which the three viewing points converge will suggest a good position for the waterfall. To help visualize the correct height for the fall, stand a post of the desired height in the spot where it will be and retreat to each of the viewing points. By experimenting in this way, it should be possible to judge whether the fall will sit comfortably in the garden or be too dominant.

The higher the waterfall and the greater the flow of water, the more powerful the pump will need to be. It is best to obtain specialist advice on this. If the pond or stream looks better without a waterfall, and it is to be stocked with fish, it is advisable to have a fountain. This will help to oxygenate the water in hot or thundery weather – the equivalent of opening a car window on a hot day.

Once the size and shape of the water feature have been decided, careful thought should be given to the

surrounding area and the structure of the waterfall. Natural rocks are really best in a Japanese-style garden, where the eye is not distracted by the vibrant colours of flowers. The different shapes and colours of natural rock take on a greater importance in such a garden. As far as possible, the rocks should be in harmony with the earth tones of the surrounding countryside.

In a domestic setting, less consideration has to be given to the safety and durability of materials used for bridges and surrounding pathways than in public gardens with their many visitors. In a coastal garden, smooth grey-blue pebbles are ideal for edging ponds and steams, while a town garden calls for randomly placed paving of slate or stone around the water feature.

Streams add movement and sound in a garden, giving the surrounding area a unique atmosphere. The tiniest stream

A naturalistic pond, with earth or pebble sides, would reinforce the *wabi* character of a less formal garden. A pond edged with stone slabs would impart a more formal ambience to a garden and could be used in close proximity to a veranda, maybe appearing from beneath it.

A sizeable stream presents a garden owner with the opportunity of incorporating a bridge of some kind into the garden; this in turn makes it possible to sit or stand above the stream and gaze peacefully into its depths.

Opposite:
This damp and shady courtyard has been transformed into a mountain scene. Wet rocks edging the small stream glow with life and reveal their subtle colours.

can be energetic and lively, with clear, sparkling water racing over smooth brown and black pebbles. In a confined area that is surrounded by solid buildings, moving water energizes the air in a beneficial way, lifting the spirits of those who own the plot. Such a stream can be created by laying a length of rubber pond liner in a trench that has gently sloping sides so that the pebbles do not roll into the bottom. At either end of the trench, judiciously placed rocks or plants should be used to hide the fact that the stream is part of a circulation system that carries water, with the aid of a pump, from one end of the stream through a pipe to the opposite end.

In a larger garden where there are trees and shrubs that already add movement to the garden, it might be pleasant to have a stream that moves in a lazy, languid fashion. On hot days the stream would enhance the restful atmosphere by introducing a feeling of gentle coolness as the water slipped through and eddied around the stems of the marginal plants.

Unless the garden plot is reasonably large, any island placed in the pond or stream should be of a single rock, or maybe a grouping of three rocks to represent the Three Buddha rocks. This is because a small pond will lose its impact and serenity if a substantial island is built using several rocks on which a tree or shrubs are planted. Such an island would make the pond resemble a section of stream. In Japanese gardens, the adage 'less is more' is particularly applicable; the less the plot is cluttered with plants and rocks, the greater the feeling of tranquillity and calm.

Bridges in small domestic gardens can look out of place unless designed with great care. A scaled-down drum bridge set at an angle over a stream and half-hidden by mountain pines will add an authentic touch to a western Japanese garden. In a plot with existing mature trees, a rustic wooden-plank bridge would be in harmony and create the *wabi* spirit so cherished by the Japanese.

If space allows, a charming idea would be to build a wooden jetty with a roof, similar to the construction in the middle of the *Musaikyō* bridge in Eihōji garden. This would create a shaded area in which to sit and meditate in true Zen spirit. What could be more pleasant than meditating in the open, sitting above sparkling water, with the gentle, cooling sound of falling water in the background and the occasional emerald-green dragonfly darting past?

The all-meaning circle:

No in, no out;

No light, no shade

Here all saints are born.

Shoichi, 1202–80, Poems of Japanese Zen Masters

Rocks and their place in history Rocks are intimately associated with Japanese gardens, their untouched, natural shapes bestowing strength and character.

ROCKS & STONES

Creating space and energy

Their weathered surfaces speak of centuries surviving the coldest winters and the hottest summers, of being whipped by fierce winds, lashed by gales and caressed by gentle morning dew. While the world evolves in often tempestuous ways, rocks remain resolute and strong, their hard surfaces miraculously playing host to velvet-soft mosses and lichens.

Ancient man believed that rocks and stones contained fearsome powers, but as civilization has transformed most people's lives, sensitivity to the strength of the earth's natural forces has diminished. In most parts of Europe, there is little cause for the weather or the forces that lie beneath the earth's crust to be feared, but in included the use of rocks. Wealthy Chinese used gardens as an aid to meditation and quiet conversation. As far back as the sixth century BC, the Taoist philosopher Lao Zi believed that gardens were a spiritual aid. He advocated the achievement of 'no-mind', which was gradually attained as a person became spiritually enlightened, and believed that as negative prejudices were shed, the spirit became less mentally confined, until a longed-for state of nothingness was reached.

Japan volcanoes are still active and parts of the country experience earthquakes. It is easy to understand why primitive people, when faced with the unleashed powers of the natural world, revered them. If they lived close to a gently smouldering volcano, they could be forgiven for thinking that some powerful god resided in its bowels.

In Japan, this reverence for nature evolved into a religion known as Shintō. People became acutely aware of the different characteristics of the elements, and each characteristic became a source of worship: for example, calm water was seen as separate from torrential water; rocks were not viewed as inanimate objects but as living entities, with a lifeforce of their own.

During the Heian period (794–1185), the Japanese came to admire all things Chinese. By this time Chinese gardens had developed into a definite style that

The Chinese for landscape, *shan shui*, means mountains and waters, which indicated the importance of rocks in Chinese gardens. Rocks and stones often dominated Chinese gardens in a way that could be overpowering, and Chinese paintings frequently portrayed craggy, energizing rocks. The Dr Sun Yat-Sen garden in Vancouver, Canada, is one of the most famous Chinese gardens in the West. Here, limestone rocks are heaped upon each other to make a forceful composition; none of the rocks is smooth, being pitted with holes and hollows. The Chinese loved this effect and would imagine that the image of an animal or bird lay in the intricate patterning.

The Japanese absorbed the Chinese style of garden and then adapted it into something altogether more graceful and elegant. Instead of using extremely rough and contorted rocks, they chose rocks and stones with a calmer nature, so that they could appreciate the sensuousness of

rocks and pebbles washed shiny by the rain. Rocks are essentially masculine and so Yang in nature, whereas water is feminine and Yin.

In Heian times, when Feng Shui, or geomancy, was first practised, it was believed that rocks were balanced by water. Feng Shui is a complicated science and yet paradoxically simple. The closer a person lives to the natural world, the more their senses become attuned to the natural rhythms of our planet. Good Feng Shui can often be felt intuitively, and Zen gardens likewise ask that the viewer allow their instinctive feelings to rise to the surface. This can feel bewildering and alien at first but it does become easier with practice.

1 **Reclining horizontal rock**
2 **Diagonally set stone**
3 **Waterfall and carp stone 'rigyo-seki'**
4 **Triangula arrangement**
5 **Crane island 'tsurujima'**
6 **Turtle 'nakajima' in water**

To appreciate a rock grouping, it is important to allow the imagination and intuition to flow. The rocks then become charged with different characters and are no longer viewed as inanimate objects but as silently pulsating entities that impart greater substance to a garden. In time, everyone can learn to feel the *qi* or 'vital breath' of a garden or area of countryside, and once aware of the negative or positive areas can then create a more balanced environment for themselves. The Chinese and Japanese believed that not only was it beneficial to live in a harmonious or well-balanced environment, it also promoted longevity. Anyone who visits a harmonious Japanese garden can feel the stress levels slip away from them, which promotes better health and well-being.

Rocks play an important part in the lives of the Japanese – they are worshipped in the religion of Shintō. A rock thought to have an especially powerful character was segregated from its surroundings with a woven rope placed around it to indicate

Using rocks to tell a story

Rocks and stones bring powerful symbolism to a Zen garden. Formations of rocks and stone may be composed to resemble a mountain range in miniature, while smaller groups can symbolize the Isles of the Blest in the Western Seas or Amida's Paradise (see pp. 16–18). Some of the most popular and powerful rock groupings in Japanese gardens are those that represent the crane and sea turtles.

its sacredness. Sometimes white sand would be strewn on the ground to show that the area around it was also holy. Prayers would be made in front of such rocks, which were sometimes of an awe-inspiring size.

Throughout the history of Japanese garden design, rocks have played an important role, and their placement evolved into a highly skilled art. Rock masters were greatly respected and their talents sought after. Their knowledge and understanding of rocks were often passed down the generations from father to son.

Rocks were used in the Kamakura period (1185–1333) to represent a dry landscape. One of the oldest examples of this type of gardening with rocks is Saihōji, or the Moss Garden. The *karedaki* garden area is in three tiers to give greater depth and perspective to the design. Its success lies in the fact that it does not look as though mankind has had a hand in its composition.

In the foreground, a large rock with a flat top is set slightly behind two smaller rocks. It is said that the great Zen garden designer Musō Sōseki sat and meditated on this rock. These foreground rocks are backed by a gentle curve of boulders of varying sizes. On the left, there is a medium-sized rock with a small, flat top and angular sides, which is covered in lichen. To its left, a smaller, more rounded stone suggests the end of a mountain range. To its right, and almost centrally placed behind Musō Sōseki's meditating boulder, is a large, dominant rock. It has planes and plateaux simulating the majesty of a great mountain. Its steep

sides convey its strong character, which is reinforced by a smoother stone placed behind it to the right. Behind this beautiful grouping, there is an ocean of vibrant green moss. Dappled sunlight filters through graceful trees on to the moss, bringing out its sensual, velvet-like qualities. The moss could be read as clear skies separating tall mountain ranges; on the far side of the moss, there is another rock composition on a raised bank resembling a mountain range. As Musō Sōseki sat and contemplated, did he see mountain range upon mountain range? Or did he see the rocky shores of an island, with a calm sunlit sea and a larger island beyond? In this grouping, the tough masculinity, or Yang, of the rock is counterbalanced by the soft, textural, feminine, or Yin, character of the moss.

We do not know whether there were trees or moss between the rock groupings in the garden in Musō Sōseki's day. However, we can be sure that the rough, perpendicular nature of the rocks would have contrasted with the smooth surface of the ground between. Perhaps Musō Sōseki meditated on the fact that everyone's life has its turbulent periods interspersed with happier times.

Another temple garden belonging to the Kamakura period is that of Tenryūji. Before it became a Buddhist temple in 1339, it had been the palace of the retired Emperor Gosago, and was known as Sento Gosho Kameyama Palace. The garden was designed on the principle of three planes: a foreground, middle ground and background. The temple buildings overlook the garden's large pond, from where the overall design can be viewed in the same way as a scroll painting is viewed on a wall.

The shoreline of the pond nearest the buildings has several inlets edged with different-shaped rocks. Most are squat with flattish heads, but now and then the scheme is broken by a taller, more perpendicular rock, creating a rhythm that enlivens the composition. Without them the design would appear dull and

somewhat static. In the centre of the pond, there is a sturdy rock island symbolizing the strong spirit of Zen Buddhism. On the far side of the pond, there is a stone grouping that has brought fame to this garden: a waterfall arrangement known as the Dragon Gate Falls, or ryūmonbaku. When this was constructed in 1339, it was a new Chinese theme based on a real fall said to be on the Yellow River. The myth of a carp leaping up the falls, like spawning salmon, was popular, and it demonstrated that through hard work much could be gained and even one's circumstances be changed. To a Zen student, the story promoted the idea that through great faith and determination, enlightenment could be attained.

The two-tier waterfall no longer flows with water, but the arrangement of rocks strongly suggests a tumbling fall. At the base of the fall, two huge, upright, oblong-shaped rocks have been set a little apart, with a third, smaller, darker rock tucked behind them. The larger rock on the right has a smooth surface of different colours. Large patches of lichen growing on it accentuate its beauty, which is reminiscent of a Chinese ink painting. At the foot of the fall, there is, reputedly, the oldest bridge in any Zen garden. It is composed of three long, flat and dynamic rocks that rest on two rocks set into the water. Taller rocks are placed partially in the water and partially on land, so linking the whole composition and masking each end of the bridge. In this way, the bridge appears to be a natural part of the whole scene. It sits comfortably in front of the

Opposite:
These undressed rocks reveal their true energy and character. A tension has been produced between them by placing them slightly apart so that the upright rock appears to be shooting out of the two smaller rocks that have just broken in half.

waterfall, making a strong horizontal line in front of the vertical planes of the two main boulders of the fall.

Beyond the garden, the hills of Arashiyama can be seen and are felt to be part of the garden design. This is known as 'borrowed scenery', or shakkei. This design device became increasingly popular as gardens became smaller. It was a way by which a garden might be made to appear larger than it actually was. This appealed to Zen Buddhists, who are trained to contemplate the Buddha's observation that nothing has an inherent existence separate from the conditions that give rise to it. Tenryūji's rock grouping resembles a Chinese-style scroll ink painting, particularly in the winter when it lies under a heavy covering of snow. The snow then represents the white paper and the dark, exposed branches, tree trunks, rocks and water appear like brushstrokes.

Rocks in abstract gardens

During the Muromachi period (1333–1573), terrible civil wars – the Ōnin wars – raged in Kyōto, which caused widescale devastation. Most buildings were constructed of highly flammable natural materials and were quickly and easily destroyed. Once peace was restored, much of Kyōto was rebuilt and a new style of garden was devised: refined and somewhat abstract dry landscape gardening, which is believed to have originated in the temples of Daitoku-ji and Myōshin-ji.

After the Ōnin wars, gardens were often sited where there were no natural springs with which to create a water feature. Today, one of the best gardens of the late Muromachi period is Taizoin garden. Here, rock groupings have been interspersed with shrubs and white gravel that represents a stream. It is very much in the style of a Chinese painting and some people believe that the famous landscape painter Motonobu Kano, who is thought to have lived at Taizoin for a period, had a hand in the garden's design.

Shrubs form a background to the garden and represent dark, primeval forests. A dry waterfall, or *karedaki*, sits naturally in front of these shrubs, its rocks merging discreetly with the greenery. Squarish rocks with a gently rounded top form the base of the fall, while darker rocks represent the water. These are small, flat and thin, arranged in a haphazard way among the large rocks so as to suggest water tumbling this way and that. Clipped mounds of shrubs planted among the rocks accentuate their ancient, quiet strength.

Dry rock gardening has never lost its appeal for those who love Zen gardens and has been successfully employed in such gardens worldwide. One of the most emulated is that of Ryōanji, which has been recreated in many western gardens, one of the most notable being the Japanese garden in Portland, Oregon.

Ryōanji is a dry landscape garden from the Muromachi period. A Buddhist temple was founded here in 1450 by the warlord Hasokawa Katsumoto. Like many warlords of his time, he had a fondness for Zen because of its emphasis on self-reliance and discipline. The temple, which was damaged during the Ōnin wars, was rebuilt by Katsumoto's son in 1488. In front of the *hōjō*, or abbot's quarters, there is an oblong space. This is surrounded on three sides with pale brown earth walls, in keeping with the love of quiet refinement, or *wabi*. The walls have a small, sloping roof of grey tiles to preserve them, and this colour is picked up in the 15 rocks that are arranged in a large expanse of white *shirakawa* sand. At the Japanese garden in Portland, the area is squarer but has the same type of sand as at Ryōanji. The 15 rocks at Ryōanji are arranged into five groups, symbolizing the story of a tigress crossing a river with her cubs (see p. 21). The largest stone is placed to the right of centre. It is the only upright stone and signifies the steadfast strength of Buddha, while all the other rocks lean in a particular direction to indicate movement. In this way, a rock can be seen as pursuing or retreating and suggests a continuous flowing movement through the oceans of sand.

chequerboard design, or *ichimatsu moyō*, of flat, rectangular stones set into deep sensuous spruce moss. Rock is usually seen as stronger and more dominant than moss but, here, sinking the stones below the surface level of the moss has reversed the roles. Shrubs growing nearby have been pruned into solid, rounded shapes that accent the moss. This area of garden is backed by tall trees growing in irregular natural shapes, balancing the rigidity of the shrubs, moss and rocks and creating good Feng Shui.

Representational rocks

Rocks are often used in gardens to resemble animals, birds or boats, or to symbolize the Buddha, the Buddha Trinity or the Mystic Isles. Rokuonji garden, with its Golden Pavilion, has many rock features, which have been greatly admired and copied. It is renowned not only for its dragon-gate waterfall and carp stone, but also for its rock island composed of a 'red pine stone', or *akamatsu-ishi*. This single stone is oblong and set slightly diagonally into the water. Placing the stone in this way harmonizes it with the surrounding area. In nature, few objects are exactly horizontal or parallel to their surroundings, and by angling the rock a natural strength has been brought to the scene.

Another of the rock groupings at Rokuonji represents the fable of Hōraito, about an island that was supported by a sea turtle; on the island was a mountain known as Horaizan. This and the other islands in the grouping have a quiet character. They

Each group of rocks is surrounded by smooth moss, creating harmony and beauty. The green of the moss helps the eye separate the rocks, which are grouped asymmetrically in uneven numbers of 7:5:3, from the sand. The dense screen of trees immediately outside the garden wall compounds the serenity of the sand and rock arrangement.

Both gardening and Zen, by their nature, have evolved with time, simply because the conditions under which they are practised have changed constantly. Neither can be static, and dry rock gardening has developed continually up to the present day. At Tōfukuji garden, Shigemori Mirei designed a rock-and-moss arrangement in 1938 that was symbolic of the power of the Kamakura period when Tōfukuji was one of the five leading monasteries in Kyōto. The most photographed aspect of the garden is the

lie low in the waters of the lake – an assemblage of rocks that appear broader rather than taller. Earth placed between the groupings is planted with mountain pines that are pruned to remain in scale with the size of each island, so retaining a sense of balance and continuity. Judiciously placed rocks, which have vertical strata, have been placed around the edge of each island to create a naturalistic atmosphere.

This design principle can be followed through in most pond and stream construction. In the real world, islands and rock formations do not have clearly defined outlines, but by placing smaller individual rocks close to stone groups, a link is made between the hard, rough character of the stone and the smooth, fluid element of the water or moss that surrounds them.

In North America and Canada, many Japanese gardens have been conceived and built since the Second World War.

Below:
This area of garden at Tōfukuji was designed this century by Shigemori Mirei. He has cleverly made the vibrant spruce moss dominate the smooth flat stones that have been set in a checkerboard style.

At the beginning of the war there were thousands of Japanese living on the West Coast of America and Canada. They saw themselves as Americans but after the bombing of Pearl Harbour most Japanese Americans and Canadians were relocated to inaccessible areas. Many of these people suffered real deprivation and hardship during the remainder of the war. The spiritual need to repair the damage this caused has resulted in many deeply spiritual Japanese gardens being created in North America.

One of the great Japanese gardens conceived through the spirit of reconciliation after the Second World War is Nikka Yuko Japanese Garden in Lethbridge, on the plains of Alberta, Canada. The rocks in this garden have helped to transform it from a flat, green field into a beautiful and spiritually uplifting garden. The site architect, Masami Sugimoto, travelled extensively throughout the area looking for suitable rocks. After a week the right rocks had still not been found, when suddenly he has been meticulously placed to break the line of the fall. The result is that the water flows smoothly until it cascades over the rough edges of the rocks, which turn it into different threads. Rocks have been placed at intervals along the gently sloping grass banks of the stream. This random placing of small boulders has been continued into the stream, so that here and there smaller, rounded rocks break above the surface of the water. This attention to detail has produced a scene that is convincingly natural.

Rocks and their place in contemporary gardens

A Japanese rock garden is particularly suited to modern urban settings; the relentless expanse of concrete and glass echoes the bleakness of a mountain range where few plants grow. A rooftop garden in New York, London or Berlin would accommodate a dry stone garden with ease. Every high-rise building in the vicinity of the garden could be treated as 'borrowed scenery' representing mountains. The difficulty of creating a water feature several floors up could be overcome by placing rocks and stones in ways suggestive of torrential waterfalls and lingering placid streams, in a dry rock garden. Rocks would be an ideal medium for connecting the hard surfaces of surrounding buildings with the immediate area around an apartment. By linking one with the other, harmony and balance would be achieved.

discovered a field with the perfect boulders. Luckily the farmer was happy to part with them. By taking infinite trouble to search out the right rocks for the garden, it has been possible to create a harmonious space that gives pleasure to many people. The flat land had to be contoured so that a dragon-gate waterfall could be devised. Large, oblong rocks with squarish tops have been placed on either side of the curtain fall. The water falls in a broad, silver band on to boulders placed at its base. A carp stone that is almost diamond-shaped has been set off-centre at the base of the fall. This symbolizes the story of the garden: that through dogged perseverance the people of Lethbridge have risen above the past and created something wonderful for their future.

In another area of the garden, a stream runs over a low cascade. This is composed of several rocks, which have been set flat side uppermost with the roughest edge facing downstream. Off-centre, a small rock with a rounded top

In parts of the Mediterranean and the western United States, summer fires have become an increasing problem. Residents are advised to make a fire barrier around their property and to grow as few fire-feeding plants as possible. A dry rock garden would be an imaginative way of making this fire barrier more attractive. Rocks would add height and interest to what might otherwise be a monotonous landscape; a sterile and blank area could be energized with the addition of carefully placed rocks and stones.

It would be wise to remember that Japanese gardens are in essence a reflection of the Japanese countryside. This is partly why there is a 'rightness' about them. When building a Japanese garden in the West, give consideration to the characteristics of the surrounding countryside. In Scotland, for example, rocks are very much a part of the natural landscape and a rock garden would not appear out of place. In the south of

England, this is not so. Here, the low, gentle hills are made of soft, white chalk. As rock groupings in this landscape could easily look out of place and contrived, the stones and rocks for a garden should be smoother and of gentler colour tones.

Understanding rocks

Before purchasing any rocks, it is a good idea to familiarize yourself with what is available at your local garden centre. Buy one stone and hammer it into several smaller pieces. Fill a tray with earth and place the broken rocks in different groups on the earth. You can experiment with your tray garden by adding representational trees and shrubs made out of paper, cardboard or plant material. Since most people do not look down on their gardens, bring your eye level with the edge of the tray to judge how the design would look if life-size. A mirror held at one side will enable you to see the design from another angle. Get used to handling the small pieces of rock. Run your fingers over the rough sides of each rock to absorb the dynamics of it. A smooth stone can evoke calm feelings while a jagged rock can make you feel uneasy. Place the rocks in triangular formations in your tray garden and move them around: you will see how one rock can, by its position, alter the dynamics of the others. It is generally considered that a balanced rock grouping is made up of rocks of different sizes.

You will see that you can manipulate perspective in different ways by positioning the rocks in various ways. A sense of distance can be created in a confined space by placing the largest rock in the foreground and the smallest at the back. In this way, you are replicating nature: objects close to you appear larger than those in the distance. Always construct a foreground and a middle ground, then finally a background. A roof garden would use the surrounding scenery as its background, while a garden abutting a blank wall might need a background if the wall is such an obtrusive and unattractive feature.

In Japanese gardens, rocks are composed of uneven numbers of stones, positioned in a triangular shape to create an asymmetrical balance – a symmetrical garden is considered out of kilter with nature. A single triangle shape may be overlapped by one or more other triangles to create a more intricate picture.

Positioning rocks

When planning your garden, list the difficulties that exist in the plot. Is the garden in shade most of the day? Does it contain trees you want to keep? Is it an awkward shape, and do any areas need disguising? All these aspects and more should be analysed and taken into consideration before placing any rocks. Mark on a piece of paper existing plants that you intend keeping, and lay a triangle or triangles over them to see if they fall into a harmonious design pattern. You may find that you have a pair of trees that would conform to an asymmetrical design when a third is added. Once the existing plantings fall into this type of design, you are ready to forge ahead with positioning your rocks. If space allows, it should be possible to position the rocks within a large triangle or several smaller, interlocking triangles. In a confined area, the rocks can be grouped into a triangular shape on their own, using perhaps three or five stones.

an abstract boat. The fourth type of rock is one that is tall and thinner than its height. Large, tall, thin rocks are used as the base stone in a rock grouping. A tall, vertical stone set among smaller stones makes the scene more interesting and natural, with the base stone acting as an anchor to the rock composition. In mountainous areas, naturally occurring rocks are never all the same size, so it would be wrong not to have a variety of differently shaped rocks and boulders in a Japanese-style garden.

Choosing and selecting rocks and stones

A few carefully composed stones have more impact than many. One pebble on a beach cannot be seen as beautiful but, once arranged on a shelf with two others, its colour and texture become apparent.

A Japanese garden designer will choose the stones and rocks that are required at a quarry. None of the rocks will be dressed – that is, they will be in the same condition as when they were first excavated. None of their rough edges will have been taken off; mankind will not have had a direct hand in shaping them. A Japanese designer would always prefer to use rocks that are local to the area because their colour tones bear some relationship to the colour of the earth in the garden that is to be developed.

Many people who plan a Japanese-style garden may live in areas where there are no rocks. In this case, notice should be taken of the colour of the earth and of the buildings in the vicinity. Perhaps local

Opposite:
The smooth surface of this rock gives it an animal sensuality that suggests it is simply sleeping beneath the Rhododendrons.

houses are roofed in slate that would suggest buying rocks of mauve and grey colour tones to link the building to the garden. Buildings constructed of materials of warm reds and browns might call for sandstone rocks.

If you are planning a rooftop garden, great consideration should obviously be given to the additional weight the building will have to support. If it is not possible to reinforce the rooftop floor so that it can hold the extra weight of rocks, fibreglass rocks are the answer. Some false rocks are modelled on real ones and can thus look reasonably convincing. It is perhaps surprising that they can prove more expensive then the real thing!

When composing stone groups, place the biggest stone in position first. Select the most attractive side of the base stone so that it faces the area from which it will be viewed most. Up to a third of the base end of the rock should be buried in the soil. This gives the rock a stable and balanced look. Once your base stone is in

Japanese rock masters believe rocks have a back, front, top and bottom. The back may be flatter than the front and the top smaller than the bottom. There are four basic rock types. First, flat, low rocks, which are used for sea turtle legs and for placing at the base of a waterfall or on either side of a stone bridge. Second, a large, squat rock that might be placed overlooking a pond as a meditating stone. This type of rock imparts a feeling of quiet strength to a garden, and evokes a calm atmosphere that might contrast with the flow of a waterfall. The third type of rock is an arching rock. This is usually wider at the bottom than at the top and, as its name implies, curves to the right or left. Arching stones are used sparingly but with great effect. At Daisen'in garden, an arching stone has been placed resting on its curved, long side so that it resembles

position, place two or four stones around it. Experiment with placing them in different positions until you feel that you have achieved a harmonious grouping that fits into a triangle. Before digging holes for these additional stones, step as far back as possible and look at the grouping from a distance. Does it sit comfortably within the whole garden design? If not, is it because you need an additional collection of rocks placed in the triangle that incorporates the whole plot? It might be that a single stone on its own strikes the right note in the garden; often a single stone can make a stronger design statement than a group of them.

When placing rocks in a pond, it is usually impossible to sink them into the bed of the pond or stream. They should be supported with smaller stones placed around their base, as long as they cannot be seen above the water surface. Japanese garden designers usually continue the rock theme from the pond to its periphery and beyond. In the wild, it is likely that where a stream or pond has rocks in it there will be a scattering of boulders nearby.

The cracks and fissures in rocks suggest the direction in which they should be placed. If the strata of a large rock run along its length, then an upright position seems appropriate. However, if it were placed horizontally, it would add a very powerful lateral dimension to the area. A rock with strata running horizontally can be used to emphasize the perpendicular nature of another rock close by.

A dry rock garden is most suitable for city gardens where permanent shadows are cast by nearby buildings, making it difficult to grow a wide selection of plants. The rocks give style and substance to such a garden, so that the success of the design is not dependent on plants. Often plants do not thrive in city gardens because of pollution and the lack of direct sunlight. In such a situation, it would be possible to design a *karesansui* garden with a dry waterfall and stream. Judiciously placed small-leaved evergreen plants would relieve the monotony of the hard surfaces, and these plants would tolerate the poor growing conditions better than perennials or deciduous shrubs. The owner of the garden would find it refreshing to make the emotional leap from the hard, relenting city streets to his or her personal mountain range, and the serenity evoked by harmoniously placed rocks would calm then revitalize the spirit.

The ruggedness of the west coast of California, for example, could easily accommodate a dry rock garden. In certain wild areas, boundary walls and hedges are not permitted, so a plot that melds with the surrounding landscape is what is required. The 'borrowed scenery', or *shakkei*, of distant hills would make a splendid backdrop for a Japanese rock garden. Where there is a natural supply of rocks, the garden would become part of the surrounding landscape and feel comfortable and restorative to be in. When a garden feels good, it counterbalances the negativity that can be felt in the world beyond; it refreshes the spirit.

Calm, activity – each has its use. At times

This worldly dust piles mountain-high.

Now the neighbour's asleep, I chant a sutra.

The incense burnt away, I sing before the Moon.

Soen, 1859–1919, Zen Poetry

Many Westerners believe that all Japanese gardens consist of vast areas of white sand with an unrelenting, lifeless character. Without understanding the importance and symbolism of sand and rocks in a Zen garden, they discount *karesansui*, or dry sand and rock gardens, symbolizing water and mountains. In fact, this type of garden has an emotional and spiritual depth rarely found in

SAND & GRAVEL

Creating simplicity and serenity

the West. To be enjoyed and understood to the full, a very different mental, emotional and even physical approach from that used to appreciate a typically Western garden is needed.

In Europe and North America, gardens are usually designed around plants and colour to excite the viewer emotionally and visually. Conversely, Japanese gardens, especially *karesansui*, are created with a completely different object in mind, namely to calm the spirit in order to promote deep contemplation.

A *karesansui* garden is the most Zen of all Japanese garden styles. Originally designed by priests whose guiding principle was that 'less is more', these gardens are, in many ways, a reflection of the spirit of Zen. As the Zen student reaches deeper insight, so he or she throws aside prejudices that clutter thinking. Similarly, *karesansui* gardens dispense with any plant or rock that is superfluous to the overall design. These gardens were, and still are, designed to enable viewers to slow down their thinking and soothe their emotions. If viewers walk quickly past such a garden, they will absorb nothing from it. The more time spent looking at these gardens, the more one will receive from them both visually and spiritually.

Raked sand adds a textural element to a garden. As the sun travels around the plot, shadows appear on one side of the raked ridges, introducing light and darkness to an area that, if brushed smooth, would

appear a monotone white. The Japanese were extremely fond of viewing gardens by moonlight, and *karesansui* gardens became almost ethereal when bathed in the silver glow of the moon.

It is no coincidence that many *karesansui* gardens were designed to be viewed from inside a nearby building – usually the abbot's *hōjō*. The longer the viewer sits and gazes, the more the spirit calms and the emotions settle. His or her heart rate may even slow down.

The less a person is used to slowing down and 'just sitting', the harder it is to benefit immediately from a contemplation garden. A person seeing a sand and rock garden for the first time may feel ill at ease, just like a person unused to looking at an abstract painting. With practice, more will be seen in the garden, and greater peace and tranquillity absorbed from it. In the frenetic lives of so many people, this type of garden has an important role to play.

Sand and its use in Zen gardens

At Ryōanji, and at many other Japanese temple gardens, *shirakawa* sand is used in *karesansui* plots. This is a type of crushed granite with angled sides, found in rivers and streams. For many centuries the Japanese have revered water as a sacred element, and anything that was strongly associated with it – a plant such as the lotus or an object that had come out of the water – was also regarded as sacred. In the early years of Shintō worship, white sand from riverbeds was often sprinkled

around a sacred stone to indicate that the ground was also holy and should not be walked on. This association continues today, so that white sand is sprinkled around notices in parks that request visitors not to walk on the grass. This use of visual unwritten messages is one that appeals to the Japanese and is understood by all ages.

Karesansui had been incorporated into large gardens of the early Muromachi period as far back as the eleventh century. These gardens were designed as an area within a larger garden to be walked around. It is thought that the first *karesansui* garden designed to be viewed from a building was built in 1499 at Ryōanji. This contemplation garden is the most well known of all gardens designed in this style.

The courtyard garden of Ryōanji occupies an oblong space in front of the abbot's *hōjō*. The natural wood planking of the veranda in front of the *hōjō* is separated

Opposite:
Finely raked curves of sand around these rocks convey a feeling of movement and energy, reminiscent of rapidly flowing water.

Below:
1 Straight and wavy
2 Island and ripple effect
3 Chequerboard effect
4 Mirroring shrubs effect

from the area of white sand by four straight bands, comprising three different textures, and framing the sand and rock composition in the same way as a picture. Adjoining the wooden floor, square slates have been set diagonally in the ground. Butting up to the dark slates there is a band of long, narrow, pale stone slabs, and, next to these, massed slate-grey rough stones are set in a random fashion. Finally, between the rough stones and the sand is another band of contrasting oblong pale stone blocks.

Fifteen stones have been set into the sand in groups of 7:5:3, conforming to the Zen idea of harmony residing in uneven numbers. Although the rocks are not set deeply into the ground, they seem stable and secure. This is as a result of their shapes, which are broad and low-standing, and the pool of moss that surrounds every rock. Each rock arrangement is encircled by evenly raked sand, separating it from the various groups. From a distance this is not obvious, but, on closer inspection, one can see that although each stone grouping is part of an overall plan, each forms a perfect design on its own. The remaining sand has been raked into broad, straight bands running the length of the courtyard. At each end a wide band of raked sand runs across the long bands. The effect of this is to add strength and power to the whole design.

1

2

3

4

This garden at Ryōgenin was partly reworked in 1980; the moss and rock island represents a sea turtle; the three rocks in the background, a crane.

The entire composition can be interpreted as the viewer wishes: the attitude he or she has towards the world will help determine what is understood, and as his or her understanding increases and changes, so the interpretation of this contemplation garden will also change. The design could be read as: each of us alone is responsible for our own actions, although these actions are in one way or another interactions with others. Another interpretation is that one good thought is both separate and yet at the same time related to other thoughts.

Daisen'in garden is considered a masterpiece of various rock and stone compositions. It is in the premises of Daitokuji, where it was traditional for the Zen monks to build gardens that they had designed themselves. It is thought that the Zen monk Kogaku Soko built the garden with his own hands in 1533. The area south of the hōjō is flat and oblong. As at Ryōanji, the sand has been raked in long, straight lines the length of the garden. At each end a broad band of raked sand runs across the long band. A narrow band of pale oblong stones, with a deeper band of slate tiles laid diagonally, encompasses the design, framing it perfectly. There are no rocks here, just two simple piles of white sand; around these the sand has been raked into gentle curves that are carried down the length of the garden, adding a graceful movement to the design. Here, the sand is said to symbolize a world of emptiness or the infinity of the ocean; the effect is one of deep tranquillity.

Another masterpiece of stone and sand in the garden of Daisen'in is an area that depicts a mountain scene like those on sansui screens. White sand represents rapidly flowing water. Just as water divides around half-submerged rocks, so the bands of sand part and flow around each boulder that lies in their path. Treated in this way, the sand brings energy and a dynamic element to the area, in contrast with the deep serenity of the timeless ocean area.

Not all karesansui gardens have their sand raked. At Kokokuji garden, the sand lies flat and smooth, with large, low-standing, smooth stepping stones set into it. The first stone is not as smooth as the rest and is known as a 'shoe removal stone', or kutsu-nugi. The stones are meant to be walked on and are a way for the visitor to reach the pond that lies beyond. Breathtaking scenery of forests and hills acts as a backdrop or shakkei ('borrowed scenery') to the sand and rock design. The calm waters of a natural reservoir behind the garden appear as an extension of the smooth sand. The densely wooded hills on the far side of the reservoir add a textural element to the scene. It is unusual for such a large expanse of water to be so close to a karesansui garden, but by keeping the sand flat, the two are in harmony with each other.

Opposite:
Swirls raked into the
sand impart a feeling
of movement and
energy that is in
contrast to the
towering solidity of the
carefully placed rocks
– so creating a
dynamic picture.

During the Edo period, Japan effectively cut herself off from the rest of the world. From 1640 until 1854, only the Dutch were allowed to land on Japanese soil, and then only on the tiny island of Deshima. Once a year the ruling shogun required a report on the state of the outside world, ensuring that Japan was aware of developments in the West while remaining mysterious to westerners. Symbolic of this isolationist attitude are Nakaniwa gardens, which are small spaces encompassed by buildings. A *karesansui* garden was ideally suited for these often damp, shaded areas. At Tōkai-an, there is a particularly fine design representing the Zen idea that the entire world lies in the most infinitesimal object. The shape of the garden is oblong, with dark, wooden buildings on all sides. Seven rocks of mottled greys and browns are laid in an ocean of grey granite chips. The seven rocks are of varying sizes and placed in a random fashion on an imaginary central line running through the courtyard. One of the smallest rocks has been placed in the

centre, its position enhanced by smoothing the sand directly around it into a circle, then raking ever-increasing circles around it to the outer limits of the courtyard.

The number seven is used in Buddhism to symbolize the compassion of the Buddha. The inference of placing a small stone in the central position could be that what is sometimes seen as inconsequential may be of the utmost importance, with far-reaching effects, or that a small kindness can have a ripple effect of huge proportions.

Karesansui gardens have continued to develop up to the present day. A particularly appealing example from the Showa period (1926–89) is at Zuihō-in. The garden has been designed south of the abbot's *hōjō* and is based on a Zen riddle. Shrubs growing in one corner are clipped to form a hedge; moss-covered earth has been piled up at the base of the shrubs, and this slopes gently down to the sand. An inlet has been created in the earth, replicating a shoreline. Perpendicular rocks have been placed from the top of the slope to spill down into the sand; some are set at a slight angle, adding a tension and liveliness to the area. A short distance from this group of rocks stands a single upright stone representing the Buddha. The sand has been raked into energetic waves throughout the entire space, and it appears that larger grains of sand, representing the spume, lie at the crest of each wave. In winter, a gentle covering of snow highlights the sand waves and emphasizes the powerful sense of movement that the garden conveys.

Japanese gardens in North America

Japanese gardens in the US are often designed and constructed in conjunction with a sister town in Japan, and usually with the help of Japanese landscapers so that they have authenticity. Most of these gardens are in public parks; some were established at the beginning of the century, but the majority have been created since 1950 in a spirit of reconciliation after the Second World War. Many American and Canadian cities such as San Francisco, Vancouver and Alberta have a large population of American or Canadian Japanese living within their boundaries who are interested in supporting the creation of a garden that belongs to the culture of their ancestors. This imparts a spirituality to them that many European Japanese gardens are lacking. In Australia, meanwhile, Japanese gardens are usually designed and built by private individuals as an garden to be encompassed on all sides by verdant green grass and on three sides by shrubs. Separating the sand-filled oblong from the guest-house veranda is a band of grass that has been broken up by the insertion of geometric stepping stones placed in a random fashion. The grass and stone continue around the garden and meld into the gently clipped mounds of shrubs. The greenery imparts a strong feeling of tranquillity and peace that is entirely in keeping with the purpose of a garden of contemplation.

extension of their other Japanese interests, which encompass the martial arts of Japan that were popular with the ruling shoguns. Unlike their American counterparts, Japanese gardens in Australia are small and privately owned, often in a courtyard.

The *karesansui* garden at Bloedel Reserve, Bainbridge Island in Washington State, US, is a development of the courtyard gardens of Ryōanji and Daisen'in. Whereas these two gardens are enclosed and confined by walls and hedges, the dry garden at Bloedel Reserve is in a relatively open site and, consequently, has an airy feeling. Just as at Ryōanji and Daisen'in, it has been designed to run lengthways in front of a Japanese-style guest house. Because of its location just off the American-Canadian coast, Bainbridge Island is a green oasis with a damp atmosphere, which has made it appropriate for the *karesansui*

Whereas the courtyard gardens of Ryōanji and Daisen'in are framed by several bands of stone and rock, at Bloedel Reserve there is a simple, continuous, narrow band of stone around the sand. The white sand has been set with seven stones placed in three groups, conforming to Buddhist design theories. Unlike the stones in the two Japanese gardens, all the rocks here are completely smooth. Facing the guest house on the left is a large boulder with its flattest side placed facing inwards. Beside it there is a round rock with straight sides and a flat top; both these rocks have been encircled by raked gravel. A small, shallow rock placed towards the centre of the garden just clips the circle of gravel. Close to the guest house, two rocks have been positioned side by side and, again, encompassed by a ring of raked gravel. The remaining two rocks have been set in the top right-hand corner of the area, also encircled with raked gravel. Lines of raked sand edge each side of the garden, emphasizing its shape. The design lies somewhere between that of the gardens of Ryōanji

and Kokokuji, for the sand is not raked over the entire surface of the plot. As the smooth sand at Kokokuji harmonized with the expanse of calm water beyond it, so, here, the flat areas of sand echo the gentle contours of the shaped shrubs and the smooth surfaces of the rocks.

Missouri Botanical Garden, or Seiwa-en – 'garden of pure, clear harmony and peace' – is the largest Japanese garden in North America. Its 'stroll-around' *karesansui* garden is an irregular shape and is edged in places by undulating clipped shrubs. The sand has been raked to emphasize the shape of these shrubs by mirroring their shape in the sand around them. The billowing pink and white azaleas just skim the sand to resemble fluffy clouds sitting on the horizon of the ocean. Rocks placed on the edge of the expanse of gravel also have their shapes mirrored with swirls of raked sand. This reinforces the design of the rock groupings. At one end of the garden, there is a flat green island containing several rocks, also surrounded by raked

Below:
This karesansui
garden at Tōfukuji is
highly controlled.
The sand has been
meticulously raked
into squares that
change in appearance
as the sun travels
around the garden.
Cloud-pruned Azalea
emphasise the
geometric design
of the garden while
softening the
appearance of the
rocks scattered
amongst them.

sand. This unifying theme adds strength to the overall design of the area and brings a true sense of harmony. As at Bloedel Reserve, the main section of sand is left smooth and flat. Both these gardens fit well into their local environment and impart a feeling of peace and gentleness reminiscent of sunny days beside a calm, still lake where the gentle breeze ripples the water around ancient rocks; days when time seems to stand still.

The Japanese garden in Portland, Oregon, US, has two sand and rock gardens, one created along the same lines as Ryōanji and Daisen'in, the other similar to the sand and rock gardens found in 'stroll-around' gardens from the Muromachi period. The oblong-shaped rock and sand garden in Portland is contained with walls that are protected on top by grey Japanese roof tiles from Nara. In Japan, the walls of a similar site would be made of plain earth but in Portland this was not appropriate, and the walls are painted a cream colour. As tall pines

the stones. There is a dynamic feeling in the spaces between the rocks, which shows how the spaces around rocks are just as significant as the placements.

In this garden, the entire area of sand has been raked in long, straight lines except for circles of sand surrounding each rock, which is embedded in an island of moss. These designs have been made possible by the fact that the *shirakawa* sand has angled sides that encourage one grain to cling to the next.

The flat garden in Portland was designed by a Japanese landscaper to contain the shapes of a gourd symbolizing happiness, and of a circle representing enlightenment and human perfection. The garden is in front of a pavilion used for exhibitions and lectures, and a long wooden veranda runs along one side overlooking the flat garden. From the veranda, the garden appears irregular in shape with sweeping inlets. At first, a local white sand was used, but it reflected the light too much so was replaced with the *shirakawa* sand, which is less glaring. A gourd-shaped island lies close to the veranda and nearby there is a smaller island in the shape of a circle. These islands are planted with drought-tolerant, green-leaved plants in a dense covering that needs little maintenance, and are edged with very short wooden poles that have been driven into the ground and cut level with the plants, helping to define their shape. The sand in this area has been raked into a broad band around each island to emphasize its shape. The remainder of the flat garden is raked in

overshadow this part of the garden, the light walls help lift the spirit of the plot.

The rocks in this garden represent a tigress who made her cubs swim across a river to test their bravery (see p. 21). The largest stone, which is upright, represents the Buddha who sacrificed himself to save them by diving into the waters. Each of the rocks has been positioned to convey a feeling of movement between them. They are placed in two groups of four and three and are set wide apart from each other. All point to the Buddha as though they are looking at him, and, in this way, great tension has been created between

Opposite: Tranquillity and harmony reign at the flat garden in the Japanese Garden of Portland, Oregon, US. The gardener's designer, Takuma Tono, has avoided the sand appearing monotonous by introducing islands of low growing shrubs and perennials that harmonise with the surrounding trees.

an intricate pattern that must take a great many hours to complete. Maintaining such a pattern in sand was a Zen ploy to enable the sand-raking monk to put personal thoughts to one side, as it is impossible to rake straight lines in the sand without complete concentration.

Long, parallel lines have been drawn in the sand here, the width of a rake apart. The area between the parallel lines has been divided into squares by raking the sand first from north to south and then from east to west. In the adjoining space the sand is raked east to west next to a square that has been raked from north to south. The resulting pattern is similar in appearance to a chequerboard, with the dominant squares changing as the position of the sun moves around the garden. The shadows cast by the sun give a definition to the design, and as the definition changes throughout the day another element can be contemplated. This beautiful garden is meant to be viewed from the veranda as well as strolled around in true Japanese style.

Opposite:

A large, gently curved rock allows water to gently flow from one pool to another. Discreetly positioned rocks meld with a planting of low growing shrubs and Ligularia tussilginea 'Aureo-maculata' that adds height and interest.

Right:

A feast of different textures meet the eye in this small garden.

The light and dark lines in sand contribute a Yin and Yang element to a garden, making it feel balanced and harmonious. In Japan, it is traditional for the man of the house to go to his garden on returning home from the office. Here, he sits and gazes at the space before him, breathing in its tranquillity before joining his family. Many westerners could emulate this practice if they had a small contemplation garden.

Karesansui gardens are popular in Melbourne, Australia, where the climate and the space surrounding homes promote designs that incorporate gravel and rocks. As the rocks from this area are a reddish-brown, the shingle and gravel used need to have a touch of brown so that the overall atmosphere is one of naturalness, harmony and calmness.

Devising a karesansui garden

When planning a dry sand and rock garden, you first need to decide whether you want the garden to be primarily for looking at, for walking around in, for sitting in, or for living in. Many city apartments have small balconies that can be forlorn, neglected places with one very sad-looking pot plant. A karesansui garden is an ideal solution to an unused restricted space that may be a focal point from the main room.

Most garden centres sell a permeable-membrane material designed to be put on earth and under a layer of mulch to prevent the regrowth of weeds. Measure the floor area of the balcony then buy sufficient membrane to cover the whole area and fold about an inch of membrane up the surrounding walls. In Japan, crushed gravel is used for karesansui gardens; in Europe and North America crushed limestone or granite 2mm in diameter should be used (this is similar to the grit sometimes given to poultry).

Enough should be purchased to cover the ground surface to a depth of 8–10cm (3–4 inches). Many balconies have a small drainage hole so that rainwater runs away and it is important that this does not become blocked.

Your local garden centre may be able to supply different-coloured crushed stone. Very white gravel or sand should be avoided unless the area to be covered is in shade, as the glare of the sun on it would be too intense. At the same time as selecting the colour of the crushed stone, you need to decide which rocks to use. Each should harmonize with the other, but not so much that they merge into one and their individual characters are lost. White marble rocks would lose their appeal if they were placed on a sea of crushed marble of the same colour. Similarly, if the walls of a balcony are

Opposite:
Mountains and water
are represented in this
small area of garden.
Powerful rocks emerge
from a sea of raked
gravel that eddies
around two perfectly
smooth semi-circles
set low into it.

painted white, a pale-coloured gravel would be preferable to white sand so that it does not merge with the walls. Alternatively, a band of black or brown bricks or tiles could be used to edge the sand-covered area, in the same way that the vast expanse of sand at Ryōanji and Daisen'in is framed by different-coloured borders.

Raked sand or gravel can be disturbed by the wind, so make a note of how windy the balcony is. If the buffeting is fairly constant, choose a raked design that is simple and easy to redo; *karesansui* gardens are raked usually every two or three weeks. The shape of your rake will determine the type of ridges you can make in the gravel. In Japan, rakes are either wooden with long handles, or a simple board with a zigzag pattern cut

along one of its long edges. The teeth of the rake need to be widely set apart and either square or oblong in shape, as these also give character to the design. If you are unable to find a suitable wooden rake or board, you can have fun devising one of your own out of several sheets of cardboard glued together, or a sheet of Perspex. In any case, a cardboard prototype will give you the freedom to experiment until you have hit on the type of rake that will produce the design you have visualized. You could then have the design copied on to a plank of wood by a carpenter or handyman.

It could even be possible to create an interesting *karesansui* area on a balcony without rocks. The interest could be supplied by raking the sand into geometric swirls and circles. From time to time, a fresh design could be devised that would aid contemplation, as the mind is less likely to wander when there is an interesting object for it to focus on.

Suburban and rural plots

In larger areas of garden, the same basic design choices have to be made as in a balcony garden. The preparation of a flat garden is of vital importance if the area is not to be a future source of difficulties. Most gardeners will begin with an area of lawn or flowerbeds that they want to transform into a sand garden. Unless all plant material is removed before beginning the garden, the site will never be flat and free of weeds. Laying a membrane on top of a lawn or flowerbed will result in an uneven surface. If you have the time, a good way of creating a weed-free area is to lay an old carpet on top of the area to be transformed – no Buddhist would want to use strong weed-killing chemicals that could harm the environment. After six months, the carpet will have smothered every weed and an area of smooth earth will be waiting to be transformed into a sand and rock garden.

Karesansui gardens do not have to be surrounded by walls, as the gardens of Bloedel and Kokokuji demonstrate. In mountainous areas, the surrounding scenery can be 'borrowed' to enhance the design of the garden. In fire-risk areas, a dry stone and sand garden can act as a fire break around the property. However, such areas are frequently very windy and it would not be practical to have finely raked sand because its pattern would be continually disturbed. Instead, patterns can be made with different grades of gravel and pebbles.

Having prepared the site well, crushed granite should be laid at least 8cm (3 inches) thick over the entire surface. Just as at Kokokuji, the surface can be left unraked and interest created by positioning rocks of a similar character to those of the surrounding landscape. These should have a broad base so that they appear to be standing firmly in the gravel. Any tough plant with a shallow root system can be planted around the

rocks to anchor them visually to the design. A contrasting border around rocks and islands could be made out of larger-sized gravel of the same type as the main section of sand. It would be a good idea to divide the larger gravel pieces from the smaller; to prevent them from becoming mixed, embed tiles in the ground, long edge downward, between the two types of gravel for a subtle effect. Borders could also be made around the site in a similar manner to frame the design and give it greater interest.

An alternative to sand is pea shingle, which does not need to be raked. Grains of shingle with sides smoothed and rounded by the constant movement of the tides will not adhere to each other. Shingle can be bought in various sizes, so it is possible to create a dry sand garden using different types of shingle to create textural differences. In areas that are exposed but not overshadowed by buildings and trees, pea shingle would provide a visually gentle composition more in harmony with the surrounding countryside than an expanse of white sand; seen from a distance, white sand would stand out like a scar on the landscape. Swirls resembling eddying water could be made around rocks using different-sized shingle, and, by separating one from the other with a barrier of stones or embedded tiles, an authentic Japanese garden can be created.

Urban dry sand and stone gardens

The *karesansui* garden at Tōkai-an shows that enclosed areas, such as urban apartments, can be made to feel light and serene. Many apartment blocks built in Japan before 1920 have a basement area, usually a few feet wide, running around the perimeter of the building. Vertical concrete walls usually entomb these sites, rendering them dank and dreary and notoriously difficult to make attractive. A *karesansui* garden suits these difficult plots because their strong visual content counterbalances the unrelenting verticals of the surrounding walls. A dry sand and stone garden can be designed to be viewed from above as well as from sideways on. Designed as an abstract painting, a *karesansui* garden loses nothing – indeed benefits – from being seen from unusual angles.

According to Zen and Feng Shui beliefs, every corner and aspect of one's environment is important and deserves respect. If a dark passageway runs around your home, transform it with gravel, a rock and perhaps an attractive pot planted with bamboo or an acer. The whole air of the area will change immediately, giving it a positive energy that will lift the heart.

Before starting work, make sure that rainwater can drain away. It is also important that any gravel laid on the existing concrete surface does not cover the damp-proof course; this is a thin line of impervious material laid between two courses of bricks. Clean the area well. If algae is growing on the walls, rub them down and wash them with an anti-fungicide. After visiting your local garden centre to decide on the colour of gravel or sand, visualize how it will look next to the existing wall colour. (If you find this

difficult to do, buy paint in a similar colour to the gravel and paint enough sheets of newspaper to lay over the entire area to be covered in sand.) It could be that your walls would benefit from a fresh coat of paint anyway. Masonry paint now comes in a wide range of colours, some available in small tester pots. It is always well worth thoroughly preparing any surface to be painted, and most masonry paints last longer if put on over a coat of stabilizer; this prevents the dampness in the wall pushing the paint away from it.

Having cleaned, stabilized and painted your walls and put a cover over any drainage holes, you are ready to construct your *karesansui* garden. The decisions now are similar to those for a balcony garden. Do you intend to rake the area and have rocks and plants? In a sunken area, wind is not likely to be a huge problem so raked gravel is a realistic option. This would provide greater interest than a simple flat surface and also provide an opportunity to show off your design skills. Most enclosed basement areas have a simple means of access, which makes maintenance easier. In Japan, this type of 'between' space often has the sand raked in lines parallel to the building, enforcing the dynamics of the architecture. It might be preferable to rake waves into the gravel to give the impression that the site is wider than it actually is. By creating a surface area that has a strong visual appeal, the eye is taken away from less attractive features. A strategically placed rock or group of rocks encircled by swirling sand would strengthen the overall design. Rocks and

plants would add height and could be used to imply a foreground, middle ground and background.

A large rock or evergreen bush placed at the forefront of the area would have the effect of pushing the back wall further away from the viewing point. This could be reinforced by placing a medium-sized rock in the middle ground and a smaller one in the background. If the design were solely of rocks and sand, without the distraction of foliage plants, it could be made to appear visually exciting from above. Obviously, the rocks would have to be attractive when seen from above as well as from the side. They should be placed as one would place marks on a sheet of paper or canvas, with regard to the spaces around each mark. In this way, a combination of tension and harmony, which is emotionally and visually appealing, can be generated.

Opposite:
An undulating expanse
of Rhododendrons and
Azaleas look their best
under a canopy of tall
deciduous trees.

Full autumn moon –

on the straw mat,

pine shadow.

Kikaku, 1661–1707

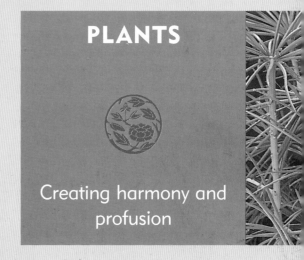

PLANTS

Creating harmony and
profusion

Plants and emotions Plants play an important part in the lives of the Japanese. Their culture has taught them to see subtle differences of colour and shape that are often overlooked by a westerner. The minute changes in colour tone of tree bark and a flower petal are fully appreciated by the people of this mountainous group of islands. The sensuous qualities of various mosses are noted and admired, and Japanese gardeners take pains to preserve and nurture these subtle variations. Attention is given to the textural qualities of plants when planning a garden so that one plant complements another – so enhancing each other's character.

In the pillow book of Sei Shonagon, tenth-century Japanese court life is portrayed as highly sophisticated, messages from one courtier to another being couched in poetic terms with frequent references to the plant world. A message could be answered with a single flower or a sprig of blossom because the symbolic meaning of them was so well understood that words became superfluous.

Every activity in the Heian period was dictated by the Japanese calendar, which was extremely complicated and vitally important as a tool of determining the most auspicious time and place for every conceivable event. The different seasons were of great importance and plants were used to highlight their differences. In this way certain plants became associated with admired character traits. A plant that was evergreen and survived the cold snows of winter was linked with courage and bravery.

The Japanese calendar was roughly one month ahead of the western calendar, with its New Year's Day falling between 21 January and 19 February. Sei Shonagon writes of three important festivals that were named after flowers. Early in the year, on the third day of the third month, the Peach Festival was celebrated. The Chinese associated the peach tree with immortality and so it became a plant of great significance to the Japanese. Two months later, the Iris Festival was celebrated on the fifth day of the fifth month. Everyone wore an iris, and in some cases an iris root; women and girls pinned them to their jackets, while courtly gentlemen decorated their head-dresses with an iris or two. The leaves of the iris were used to decorate the eaves of houses and were believed to bring good fortune and frighten evil spirits away. The third flower festival was named after the chrysanthemum and was observed on the ninth day of the ninth month. On this day, bunches of chrysanthemums were tied to the wooden pillars of buildings as a protection against evil winter spirits. This flower was considered sacred and was associated with purity. A Buddhist story tells of a youth who was entrusted with some holy texts, which he painted on to the petals of a chrysanthemum; dew from the petals then became imbued with special powers. Sei Shonagon relates how the qualities of dew were much admired by some courtly ladies, who allowed the grass in their garden to grow unfashionably long in order that they might enjoy the early morning sun shining on the dew-drenched grass blades.

The Japanese people's love of the understated was derived from their deep affection and reverence for nature. They felt that there were unseen natural forces around them that could be altered and improved by the judicious placing of plants. In addition, by using plants in a symbolic way, a person was reminded of the significance of their spiritual life. Weaving symbolic elements into a garden gave it a deeper dimension that could be appreciated on an emotional and an intellectual level. This additional, intangible element compensated for the lack of many flowering perennials in their gardens and in the long term helped to create a garden that had a subdued, mysterious quality.

Opposite:
The purple veins of
the Japanese iris
only add to its beauty.
It stands up to
20–60cm (8–24 inches)
tall on the margins
of ponds and streams
where it flowers
profusely during
mid-summer.

Perennial plants are not usually grown in Japanese gardens for a number of reasons. Gardens were originally designed to imitate nature, and since flowerbeds do not appear in the wild they had no place in a Japanese temple garden. Mass planting of mixed perennials would have detracted from the quiet beauty of moss-covered ground and the reflective mood of shrub and tree groupings. Perennials were seen as too transient in the growth pattern, and it is because so few were used that centuries-old gardens have retained their original character. The Japanese loved the strong, stable qualities of shrubs and trees, as these elements were often missing in their personal lives.

Japanese gardens are designed to be complete when they are first built, not to evolve over the passing years as western gardens are so often expected to do. Trees and shrubs were, and still are, controlled by clever pruning, making it difficult to tell how old some are because they remain in the same shape from one year to another. In this way, the picture

the garden presents is reassuringly familiar from one year to another. A garden that retains a certain look and style over the passing years becomes like a reliable friend. The visitor can be certain that a favourite grove of trees will be comfortingly the same. The moss around the roots of the trees will still resemble velvet in the soft sunlight that filters through the tree canopy. Shrubs that delighted the visitor as a child with their cloud or sea turtle shapes will be there to be enjoyed by their children. In a world that changes daily, it is heartwarming to return to a loved, familiar friend. A Japanese garden is similar to a painting that continues to give pleasure even when every brushstroke is known. Returning to a garden that retains the same look from year to year gives the visitor a sense of peace on a deep level. Visitors may feel agitated and overexcited owing to events in their lives, but on entering a Zen garden, and allowing its understated elegance and quiet refinement to enfold them, a sense of peace and tranquillity pervades their souls.

Flowering plants are used in Japanese gardens to call attention to the time of year. Flowering azaleas signal to the visitor that spring has finally arrived and the harsh bleakness of winter is past. Purple and white Japanese iris flowering under the clear, blue skies of summer seem to balance the intensity of the sky, bringing an added harmonious thread to the garden.

In autumn the vivid colour of acer leaves announces that the days are becoming shorter and that soon their branches will be bare against the winter frosts. In this way, plants can provoke nostalgic thoughts of past springs or autumns when important life events occurred.

The dominant colour in Zen gardens is green, but the entire range of green shades and tones are used. It is only possible to create an interesting plot using one dominant colour when plants are familiar and their habits understood. Mixing shrubs and trees that have leaves of a different shape and size from each other provides variety. In this way, textural differences that provide subtle variations are incorporated. Each type of deciduous tree or shrub will come into leaf at a different time and this in itself provides visual stimulation and interest. Some leaves open as a pale, shimmering sea-green colour that darkens with age; others unfurl into richly apple-green shades that become more muted with the passage of time. Few leaves remain the same shade of green throughout the growing season and, with an intimate knowledge of the trees and shrubs to be used in a plot, a deeply appealing planting plan can be devised.

Leaves differ not only in their shape and colour but also in their light-reflective quality. The Japanese gardener is adept at manipulating this quality when pruning a plant. The intention is to enhance and accentuate the plant's true character, retaining the natural shape of the shrub while pruning out any branch or twig that obscures the underlying form. This is called 'feather pruning' and, when carried out with skill, it results in a shrub that has a beautifully shaped basic structure of trunk and branches overlaid with a delicate covering of leaves that resembles a lace mantle.

Pruning

When shaping a tree or shrub, careful consideration is given to how the sunlight falls on to and through the plant. The idea is to allow the sunlight to illuminate the leaves so that the tree or shrub does not appear as a solid mass. An *Acer palmatum* (maple) growing in a clearing that is surrounded by evergreens becomes more alive to the eye when the sunlight can filter through the branches to illuminate the leaves. The effect is particularly lovely in the autumn when the leaves of the acer become suffused with crimsons that glow against an evergreen background. Acers are particularly well suited to feather pruning and the more cut-leaf varieties become breathtaking in their beauty when handled in this way.

By thinning the leaf canopy of a shrub or tree, sunlight is allowed to illuminate the ground beneath the plant gently. This enables sensuous mosses and other groundcover plants to grow in the soft light that falls through the delicate leaves above. Gentle shadows are more appealing than solid, heavy ones. They have a lighter mood that is beneficial to the overall character of a garden. Solid blocks of shadow have a sombre mood that can be intimidating and threatening at times. Heavy shadows mask the beauty of tree trunks and small plants growing at ground level; they are also in strong contrast to bright sunlight. This polarization of light and dark can feel uncomfortable as well as be hard on the eye. A garden filled with dappled sunlight is romantic and enticing; dancing

shadows lift the spirit and are easy on the eye. Often, when working out the planting plan of a garden, little thought is given to the powerful impact that shadows can have. The length of shadows cast will vary with the time of year and the angle of the sun. The brighter the sun, the stronger the shadows will be. In hot climates, shadows provide a cool oasis away from the glare of the sun, and by planting trees and shrubs that have densely leafed canopies, solid blocks of shadow can be created as an additional design element. If feather-pruned shrubs are placed around a tree that is densely leafed, gentle dappled shadows will result that provide a transitional stage between the sunlight in the open space of the garden, and the inky depth beneath the tree, creating an effect similar to the Chinese ink paintings that were admired by the Japanese.

The branches of this pine have been lovingly tied to bamboo poles so that they grow at the desired angle in order to mimic the pines in scroll paintings.

In *karesansui* dry gardens, this is an element that should be considered when planting the plot. An expanse of gravel is very like a sheet of drawing paper that only comes to life when ink or paint has been placed on it. Since dry contemplative gardens have a more static nature than 'stroll-around' gardens, shadows from nearby plants introduce a variable element that is both interesting and attractive.

Pine trees are intimately associated with Japanese gardens. They have long been highly respected for their longevity and refined character, while their straight, evergreen needles or leaves were another indication of their proud spirit and courage in surviving the harshest of winters. Pine trees have a dignified aura and are never ostentatious, traits that the Japanese admire.

Chinese artists had incorporated weathered pines into the decorative paintings that adorned objects and scrolls. As gardens became more abstract in style, the pine became more stylized. A tree seen from a distance becomes a simple outline and the intricacies of its shape cannot be seen; it was this long-distance view that was replicated in Chinese art. 'Cloud pruning' (see p. 104) a pine gave it the simple shape that can be seen in willow-pattern designs. To westerners this can seem strange. During the twentieth century in Britain there has been little inclination on the part of gardeners to train the branches of their trees into a more visually pleasing shape. In Italy, Holland and Germany, though, there is a greater tradition of snipping and clipping shrubs and trees that dates back to the Middle Ages, when shaping plants was a skilled art. With gardens becoming increasingly smaller, it is more important than ever that the few shrubs and trees growing in them should be of a pleasing shape and density.

Pines lend themselves to being shaped. A Japanese gardener does this by tying lengths of bamboo to each branch that he or she wants to bend in a certain direction. The bamboo poles are lovingly tied to the tree with lengths of black cord. This is in the spirit of Zen Buddhism, which teaches that every act should be done beautifully and with love. The bamboo pole is kept tied to the branch until it has grown firmly alongside the pole, which usually takes from two to three years. The pines' flower candles are removed so that none of their strength goes into making cones. This practice also allows the gardener to prune or trim the whole tree, even adjusting the lengths of leaves. Shaping the tree in this way can give the impression that it is much older than it is; since the Chinese and Japanese thought that the pine could live for a thousand years, a weatherworn, aged tree is much prized.

Opposite:
Japanese Holly with its
small evergreen leaves
is suited to being
clipped and trained
into the comforting
'cloud style' so typical
of Zen gardens.

Pruning gives the gardener the opportunity to put aside his or her problems and concentrate on the job in hand – thinking only of the branch that he or she is tying to a length of bamboo, all troublesome thoughts have to be laid on one side in order to give the care necessary to the tree. By caring for the tree or shrub in a loving manner, the gardener is very likely to have a flash of inspiration that will resolve a difficulty that may have been unresolved for some time.

Japanese garden masters did not use plants that were unfamiliar to them. They used their native trees and shrubs, whose needs they understood, to create gardens that were and are in sympathy with their mountainous countryside.

Going with nature

The Moss Garden at Ryōanji may not have originally been planted with moss, but because of the damp climate little else could grow under the trees that had been planted. To fight against nature's inclination to clothe the ground in moss would have been futile. By going along with nature, harmony is created and, in the process, a relaxing place emerges in which a person's inner self can rise to the surface.

This can be seen in the Japanese garden of Portland in Oregon, US, where existing Douglas firs and Western Red cedars have been woven into the garden's overall design. Portland is fortunate in that its soil is acid, as is the soil in most native Japanese gardens, so plants that originated in Japan, and that are closely associated with the accepted look of a Zen garden, can be grown easily there. The climate of Oregon has also played a part in the success of Portland's garden, the winters being usually wet with some heavy snowfalls. A wide range of plants can be grown successfully in this usually gentle climate, which again has made it possible to plant the garden in an entirely Japanese style. The native pine *Pinus contorta* (Beach pine) has been planted with European varieties such as *Pinus sylvestris* (Scots pine), and the tough *Pinus mugo* (Dwarf Mountain pine) from central Europe. Almost 30 different rhododendrons have been planted throughout the garden and their shiny, smooth leaves complement the spiny needle–leaves of the pines. All too often

rhododendrons are only appreciated when they are in full flower and the beauty of their new growth passes unnoticed. The leaves of this plant vary quite widely from one variety to another, and many are alluringly sensuous when unfurling. At this stage of their growth, some have a soft down on the undersides of the leaves that can be silvery-grey touched with bronze or gold; even the pale green leaf-bracts can be attractively tinged with vermilion. No doubt Zen garden masters noticed these subtleties.

Blossom trees and flowering shrubs

As the Portland garden has been designed as a 'stroll-around' garden, thought has been given to providing blossom trees that can be admired in the same way as they would be in Japan. One of the most beautiful is a weeping cherry (*Prunus subhirtella* 'pendula') that is planted on one side of the flat garden. Its leaf canopy is broad and flat, it overhangs the white raked sand, and in spring it is a cloud of sugar-pink blossom are cloud pruned so that they resemble the pines in Japanese and Chinese art. In winter, the smaller pines are protected from heavy snowfalls by wigwams of ropes attached to a central pole. These 'snow guards', prevent the snow building up on the branches, which could result in serious damage, either breaking the branch or bending it out of shape. In Japan, these guards (known as *yukizuri*) are stylish and have a charm of their own that does not detract from the beauty of the tree they protect from snow or hot sunshine.

Pines in the garden

Japanese garden designers place plants in a garden to suggest the plant's natural habit. A pine that grows naturally in mountainous areas will be used in a rock grouping to reinforce the impression that the viewer is looking at a mountain range. A pine that normally enjoys growing beside lakes and streams might be planted beside a dry stream to imply that cool, clear water is racing under its spreading branches. Two of the most frequently used pines that are native to Japan, the Japanese Red pine (*Pinus densiflora*) and the Japanese Black pine (*Pinus thunbergii*) are easily available, but others can be substituted. In Europe, an alternative to the symbolically female Japanese Red pine could be the Scots pine, but other red-barked pines are available, such as *Pinus massoniana*, and a very lovely elegant pine that is happier in warmer districts, *Pinus patula*. *Pinus contorta* (Beach pine) grows naturally on sandy soil and dislikes alkaline soil; it is a particularly attractive medium-sized tree

that trembles in the gentle breeze. It has been positioned to be viewed from the veranda of the nearby pavilion, and from here its delicate blossom stands out against the dark green of *Pinus thunbergii* (Japanese Black pine) and clipped mounds of azaleas (rhododendron hybrids).

Some Japanese gardeners trim their flowering bushes so that they do not flower, and so retain a subdued or *wabi* character all year. At Portland, the azaleas are clipped into tight mounds that become a solid mass of flowers in early summer. Trimming shrubs in this way is known as 'cloud pruning', because the plant loses its natural shape and takes on the character of a billowing cloud. When in flower, Portland's undulating pink azalea bushes remind the visitor of spectacular evening clouds that are lit up by a scarlet setting sun. By association, this leads to the thought of a heavenly place existing above the sunlit clouds.

Many of the pines in this lovely garden

that can be shaped easily. A dwarf variety, 'Spaan's Dwarf', is slow growing and has densely growing luscious, green shoots. A small dry stone garden should have a pine that has attractive 'leaves' and bark; *Pinus bungeana* (Lacebark pine) is ideal, as it is a small-to-medium tree with grey-green bark that peels to reveal a mottling of white, yellow, purple-brown and green. One of the toughest of the small pines is *Pinus mugo* (Dwarf Mountain pine), which grows happily in any soil, even alkaline; 'Winter Gold' has foliage that turns quite yellow in the winter. One of the most weather-resilient large pines is the Austrian pine or *Pinus nigra*. It will survive salt-laden air blowing in from the ocean, and for this reason is ideal as a protective wind-shelter belt; this black-barked pine is symbolic of male energy in its protective capacity. One of the best pines to grow in a Japanese-style garden is *Pinus parviflora* (Japanese White pine), which is the pine depicted on willow-pattern china. It is a small-to-medium tree whose natural inclination is to become more flat topped with age; the leaves are attractively

Opposite:
The ruby red of this
Acer palmatum is a
welcome addition to
a simple planting of
bamboo and Hosta.
Its vivid colour
counterbalances the
dark wood of the
path's edging and
brings harmony to
the area.

greeny-blue on the outside and blue-white on the inside. There are many different varieties of this valuable tree, making it possible for most gardeners to find one that suits their needs.

Pines give a garden structure and form, which becomes vitally important in winter when deciduous trees are bare. They are at their most picturesque when blanketed with snow, with a dramatic ink-black sky overhead.

At Compton Acres in Dorset, England, trees and shrubs are not as rigorously pruned as at Portland. Close to a scarlet-lacquered tea house is a most attractive pine. It is not very tall and stands on the edge of the large pond leaning slightly towards the tea house in a stylized, windswept manner. It is pruned so cleverly that its shape seems entirely natural. Azaleas in this garden are allowed to grow in a looser way than those at Portland or in some Zen gardens in Japan. This is compatible with the English way of gardening, which is renowned for its

relaxed and informal character. English visitors to Compton Acres do not feel emotionally alienated when they stroll around the garden, which they might do if the plantings were sparser and more controlled. Zen gardens have never been designed to make the visitor feel uncomfortable, their aim being to relax a person so that they may grow spiritually. In this respect, Compton Acres is successful because the emotional needs of the visitor have been reconciled with the desire to create a garden that is oriental in style.

It is well to remember that Japanese garden designers planted their gardens with plants that were suited to their climate and soil. It is only possible to create a Zen-style garden on alkaline (lime) soil if substitutes are used for the many *acers*, rhododendrons, *pieris* and camellias that are commonly grown on acid soil. This can be achieved when the qualities of acid-loving plants and how they are used is understood.

Designing a Zen garden

The western gardener can approach designing a Zen garden in two ways. The first option is to copy a typical Japanese garden slavishly, which can result in a space that feels at odds with its surroundings. The second option is to understand the essence of a Zen garden and to create an area that in atmosphere is tranquil and peaceful yet is composed of plants that commonly grow in the vicinity of the plot. The second option is more likely to be followed in climates

unlike that of Japan, and where the soil precludes the growing of typical Zen plants.

Acers are very much associated with Japanese gardens, and their lace-cut leaves bring a delicate beauty to any garden. Although one or two varieties can grow on alkaline soil, it might be preferable to use substitute plants that will provide good autumn colour and which do not object to being shaped.

Viburnums are not as delicate in leaf or as varied as the *acer*, but many are tough growing and have good autumn colour, with the addition of clusters of fruit that are attractive to birds. One of the most attractive *viburnums* is *sargentii*, which has well-shaped cut leaves that colour effectively as winter approaches. It is a hardy shrub able to withstand temperatures as low as to −30°C (−22°F). In the wild in Japan and China, it grows by streams and on the edge of woodlands, its white flowers turning into it would be respected for its ability not only to retain its leaves throughout the winter but also to flower.

Another plant that provides good autumn colour is *Euonymus alatus*, a native of Japan and China, where it flowers in May and June. Its leaves turn first to pink and then to crimson – these complement the purplish seed capsules that contain orange berries. For smaller gardens the American variety, 'Compactus' is good, formimg a slow-growing bush.

red berries in autumn; a good variety is *Viburnum sargentii* 'Onondaga'. In Britain and parts of Europe, *Viburnum opulus* 'Xanthocarpum' is a good alternative; it is a plant with a similar leaf to those of *sargentii* but the berries are a pretty, creamy yellow. It needs plenty of space if it is to grow to its full height of 5 metres (16 feet) but if space is limited, 'Compactum', which requires half the space, is an alternative.

Where camellias cannot be grown because the climate is too hot and dry, one of the evergreen *viburnums* could be substituted; *Viburnum tinus*, which is native to the Mediterranean, would be ideal. Its twigs are an attractive reddish tone, and the leaves a good shape and a rich dark green. In mild areas, during the winter months, flat flowerheads bring a joyful feeling to a plot. If it could grow in Japan,

A wonderful shrub to grow for autumn colour on alkaline soil is *Amelanchier lamarckii*, which can be clipped and trained into quite dense shapes, although the snowy flower racemes that smother the branches in spring look most attractive on naturally spaced branches. This shrub's natural inclination is to be bushy without being overpowering, which is in keeping with Zen preferences. Planted with others, it could be used to suggest a copse or wood and, because it does not resent being trimmed, it could be kept to the size required.

A delightful evergreen shrub that is native to Japan is the Japanese holly or *Ilex crenata* 'Golden Gem' or 'Golden Tip'. Do not be deterred from growing it by its name, for in reality it is more like *Lonicera nitida* 'Baggesen's Gold'. Both have tiny, yellow-green leaves and both can be shaped by trimming and clipping. *Ilex crenata convexa* 'Gold Tip' is a free-flowering shrub that in autumn is covered with small ebony-coloured berries. There are various forms of *Ilex crenata* and, with

more appearing on the market, most gardeners should find at least one variety of this fully hardy shrub to suit their plot.

In Mediterranean climates, where the humidity can be too low for rhododendrons and acers to grow, substitutes should be chosen that have the qualities that Zen designers admire: evergreen leaves, longevity and a subdued character. Pointed leaves are usually avoided, in preference for a rounded shape. It is a mistake to think that water and winter temperatures are the only factors to consider when choosing plants. A plant that naturally grows in a damp

Prunus 'Okame' is a lovely, small cherry tree that is covered in rich, rose-pink flowers during March and has attractively coloured foliage in the autumn.

atmosphere will not be happy with water supplied only to its roots. A pond nearby will provide additional humidity but this may not be enough for some azaleas and rhododendrons. In areas of intensive sunlight that have a dry atmosphere, a hedge of oleander (Nerium oleander) would give the same colour impact as cloud-pruned azalea bushes, and its evergreen leaves would provide the same year-round restrained atmosphere that is so important in Zen gardens.

Olive trees have many qualities that are admired by Zen garden masters. They are long lived, are happy to be pruned and are evergreen. Their personality is more suited to dry, hot situations than are rhododendrons, and their pale silver-green leaf colour adds a cool element to a sun-parched patch. Since Zen gardening is designed to reduce stress levels, it seems sensible to plant trees and shrubs that will not struggle for survival and in the process cause the garden owner hours of worry.

A tree that can become diseased as a result of pruning at the wrong time of year is the prunus. For this reason attention should be given to the ultimate size of the variety to be planted, as some can reach great heights. In Japan, there is a tradition of planting trees and shrubs that are fully grown but in Europe this is rarely done. Imagination is needed to visualize how a tree, that perhaps is only 1.8 metres (6 feet) tall in the nursery, will look when it is 9 metres (30 feet) tall. It will have grown not only taller, but also wider and denser. This will in turn result in more dominant shadows being cast over the garden, which might alter the balance and mood of the whole area. As a tree spreads, fewer plants can be grown under it, as less sunlight and rain reach the area around the front of the trunk.

A blossom tree to lighten any heart during the long, bleak winter months is Prunus subhirtella 'Autumnalis', for its fluffy, pale pink flowers withstand the coldest days from November until April, only becoming brown when drenched with rain. It has the brave spirit that is so admired by Japanese people. In autumn, the leaves of this small tree turn gold and scarlet, with the flowers opening shortly aftewards.

Groundcover

One of the greatest differences between Zen gardens and the average western garden is the management of groundcover. Lawns are not part of the Japanese designer's palette. Kyōto has a climate that is ideal for moss growing but not for the planting of lawns. In the garden of Saihōji, or the Moss Garden, where there are more than 40 different mosses, the climate here is damp, making it easy for the mosses to grow profusely in the dappled shade cast by a variety of trees. Sunlight filtering through the tree canopy illuminates the mosses, making them glow like a carpet of emeralds, reminding the viewer of the jewel-covered trees on the Mystic Isles of the Blest (see p. 16).

In the West, most gardeners are unable to grow moss successfully. With perseverance, a gardener could encourage moss to establish itself by watering the ground with a fine spray every day, but may take up to three years of watering to produce a satisfactory covering of moss. And when water is scarce this practice is questionable – would a Zen garden master strive so hard to alter the microclimate of his garden? The Buddhist way is to take account of and to respect the conditions provided. There are good alternatives to moss that are more suited to plots in the West, which can be quite dry. Designers of the Japanese garden of Portland, Oregon, US, have experimented with covering its flat garden islands with dianthus and thymes. Both are good groundcover plants if an area is not going to be trodden on. Thymes are tough and

drought-resistant plants that spread quickly. This is also a consideration, as most gardeners want to establish a type of groundcover quickly and at a reasonable cost. *Ophiopogon japonicus* can be planted as a substitute for Japanese grass, but it can be slow to establish, making it necessary to plant a greater number of plants at the outset, which increases the cost to the gardener quite considerably. If a native plant such as thyme is planted, the ground is clothed more rapidly and at far less cost. In moist, shadowy situations, baby's tears, also known as mind-your-own-business (*Soleirolia soleirolii*) is an acceptable alternative to moss. It is loathed by many gardeners because once it has established itself it is difficult to eradicate. It is composed of shiny, verdant, tiny leaves that are not always frost hardy. However, if it is damaged by frost it is quick to recover and will soon be rampaging through dank corners again. It will tolerate a little walking on and will always renew any foot damage quickly.

A delightful groundcover plant, but which can be invasive, is *leptinella*. This has feathery leaves that can be a rich purple-brown (*Leptinella* 'Platt's Black') and have a subdued character appropriate to a Japanese garden. This charming plant comes from South America and Australasia, where it grows in rocky areas and on sub-alpine grasslands. It seems to be relatively drought tolerant, which is in its favour in areas where water is becoming a precious commodity. It will also withstand the occasional walking on since its leaves are not glaucous or

Opposite:
This garden corner has so many different leaf textures and colours that the absence of flowers goes unnoticed. The large blue-green Hosta balances the delicate leaves of Acer, Conifer and grass while complimenting the lichen-smattered rock.

fragile; it is therefore suited to those areas of the garden that border paths and seating areas.

There are a number of good perennials or low-growing shrubs that provide attractive groundcover under trees or between larger shrubs or stones. A plant that is classified as a shrub, but seems more like a perennial, is the evergreen *Pachysandra terminalis* that originates from Japan. It prefers an alkaline-free soil and can be a robust plant when placed in a situation that suits it. In the north-west of the United States, it will tolerate growing in full sunshine but in hotter climates strong sunlight will turn its glossy, dark-green leaves yellow; in such conditions it is happier spreading itself among trees and shrubs.

Bamboo and grasses

Bamboo is the third of the plants most revered in Japan, as it is associated with the moon, is long lived and is often evergreen. To grow well, most bamboos appreciate a moist climate and to be placed in semi-woodland conditions. The soil should be slightly acid and well drained, and the situation should preferably be south facing. Dwarf bamboos (*Sasa grass*) grow best in shade; their leaves tend to wither in winter, so it is wise to choose one of the evergreen varieties. Many bamboos have invasive root systems that can be hard to control. They can make good shelter belts when planted on the perimeter of a garden, where they slow down the wind as it hits a garden. Hedge bamboo (*Bambusa multiplex*) is ideal for a tall hedge, as it grows to 15 metres (50 feet). Planted in clumps and as windbreaks, they bring sound to a plot as even the gentlest breeze rustles their leaves. It is this quality that makes bamboo valuable to the gardener. Grown in pots and placed on a patio or on decking, they bring the sound of ocean waves breaking on the seashore within listening distance of even the most land-locked or urban home. The joy of container-grown bamboos is that they can be rearranged to create a new picture from time to time. Pot-grown bamboos are easier to divide and control, as there is no way that they can take over the garden. A good choice would be *Sasa veitchii*, a decorative evergreen bamboo of 1.5 metres (5 feet) that has a strongly oriental personality. Its leaves are long and have a white margin, and contrast

attractively with its purple stems. The alternative to growing a bamboo is to grow one of the taller clump-forming grasses such as *Miscanthus sinensis* 'Zebrinus', which grows to about 1.2 metres (4 feet). As it develops, yellow stripes appear that gives it its name, zebra grass. The *Miscanthus* family is reasonably extensive; before choosing one to grow, visit a botanical garden, where it will be possible to see different types realizing their full height, which they can never do when grown in a nursery pot.

When planning a Japanese garden, it is worth contacting your local Japanese garden society. Most enthusiasts are generous with their acquired knowledge and are usually happy to show off their own gardens. As you walk around a Japanese garden created in the West make a note of how different areas make you feel, and take note of which plants are growing. You will learn in this way which plants thrive in the type of conditions that you will be able to offer, and thereby make a more informed choice of plants.

A perennial that naturally likes woodland situations is the genus *Epimedium*, some of which are evergreen. This plant has attractive heart-shaped leaves that range from mottled yellow-green and maroon to glossy apple-green. Mottled evergreen leaves provide colour at ground level that is welcome in the winter months when the surrounding trees and shrubs have lost their leaves. *Epimedium acuminatum*, *davidii* and *Epimedium* × *warleyense* have evergreen leaves that are tinged with either maroon, copper or red at different times of their growth. This plant likes a moist situation that is protected from cold winds. In colder places, the ground-loving periwinkle (*vinca*) would be a good alternative, providing one of the smaller-leafed varieties such as *Vinca minor* 'Gertrude Jekyll' is chosen, with its little white flowers. This is a plant that has an unobtrusive nature and a tough character, two qualities admired by the Japanese.

Shrine gate

through morning mist –

a sound of waves.

Kikaku, 1661–1707

Incorporating architectural styles The architecture of Japanese temple gardens is so distinctive that it can be recognized wherever it appears. Its definite personality requires that the westerner incorporates it with skill and care into his or her plot. It is best to position any large structure, such as a tea house, some little distance from existing buildings. So that it sits comfortably in the garden, shrubs

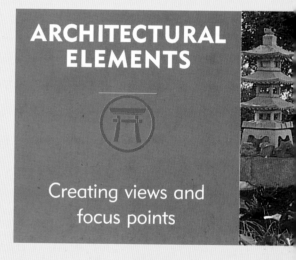

ARCHITECTURAL ELEMENTS

Creating views and focus points

should be placed around it, just as a rustic building would appear in a mountainous area in Japan. In this way, it is made is believable and not incongruous.

A veranda could be made in tune with Zen principles by placing large pebbles with pleasingly smooth surfaces, among pot-grown bamboo. Instead of the wood being painted with gloss paint, it could be allowed to develop its own natural patina, so that the beauty of the wood grain may be appreciated.

Zen-style paths would be an asset to any western garden. Their gentle curves and natural styles introduce a comfortable and relaxing element to any plot. A zigzag or plover-style path (see p. 131) could be used to give the impression that a small space is larger than it actually is, for it would take a little longer to walk it than an austere straight path.

Bamboo screens and gates add a Zen touch to a plot without overpowering it. Most western gardeners use bamboo sticks to train annual climbers, and a bamboo screen would easily harmonize with them while also adding interest.

The evolving nature of architecture

The architecture of Japan is powerful in its simplicity of style. Until the emergence of the Bauhaus school of architecture during the 1920s in Germany, the West had nothing that could compare with it. To the western eye, the Japanese

management of space, of light and of dark, together with the use of strong verticals and horizontals, seem to belong to the twentieth century.

From the earliest periods of Japanese history, a reverence for the beauty of natural objects dominated all aspects of building design. Shintō shrines were usually in remote mountainous areas, where the intangible force of nature could be felt. It became the custom to build a small building in the vicinity of the shrine to give shelter to meditating worshippers. These hermitages were rustic affairs, which harmonized with the surrounding woods or rocky terrain; their walls were of compressed earth left unadorned, and the roof would be of a deep thatch that brought warmth in winter and coolness in summer. Farmhouses were built with similar materials, and it was only the wealthy who built palaces in the more ornate Chinese style. The Japanese were conscious that certain styles of architecture were suited to the different classes that made up Japanese society. Sei Shonagon comments in her pillow book that it was most appropriate for a woman who lived on her own to do so in a dishevelled, thatched house. She clearly felt that a house should reflect one's power and status in the world.

The Japanese people's sensitivity to nature, and their acute awareness of unseen powers in the earth beneath their feet and in the air around them, influenced the positioning of architectural features. This belief in geomancy was reinforced by the introduction of Chinese

Feng Shui. Kyōto was built with the protective mountains behind it, which was considered good Feng Shui. Rivers, whether artificial or natural, were required to run from east to west, and it was thought to be most auspicious for ponds to be placed in front of a building that ideally faced south. Nature was seen as a force to be worked with rather than conquered.

Westerners have designed their homes, and especially their places of worship, to shut out the natural world. In contrast, the Japanese have always endeavoured to bring the outside in and the inside out, to create a harmonious environment. The climate of Japan aided this desire, making it possible to devise ways of unifying the garden with the temple or home. Buildings were designed with partitioned walls that could be slid aside when appropriate. With an entire portion of wall removed, the space of the room

Opposite:
Here at Ryōanji, subtle architectural elements used collectively have produced a tranquil, ageless quality. The unpainted wood of the buildings is undemanding and blends beautifully with the fence of tied bamboo bundles and the natural planting close by.

Each unadorned element in this garden has been used with loving care. The wooden walkway and bamboo fence bring warmth and beauty to the abstract arrangement of sand, rocks and shrubs.

then flowed outwards to the garden. This unifying of inside with outside was further enhanced by various design strategies. During the Heian period, when Chinese art was slavishly admired, scrolls depicting mountainous scenes were hung within a room to mirror the miniature mountain scene created in the garden close by.

Another design device to bring the two spaces together was to extend the interior wooden floor of the temple or house to the outside to form a veranda. At Rokuonji, the Golden Pavilion, the veranda has been continued out past the shadows of the eaves to form a *sosei*, or covered jetty, that projects over the water near by. A waterside pavilion or small building was originally a Chinese idea, but at the Golden Pavilion there is one executed in a Japanese style, with the *sosei* made of simple wood supported by natural rocks. A plain roof with no intricate detailing has the effect of anchoring it more intimately to the water.

On another side of the Pavilion, the raised wooden veranda drops down to a smooth, plain, wooden step and then to a broader paved area that echoes the strength of the veranda's unadorned floorboards. The darkness of the wood counterbalances the lightness of the paving slabs. The ability to interplay light with dark is part of the Japanese designer's palette and is used brilliantly here.

For hundreds of years, Japanese buildings have been designed to a measurement that is based on the human scale. The *tatami* mat measures 90 × 180cm (3 × 6 foot) and is still used in most homes as a floor covering. It is so much part of the basic measurement of a building that the size of houses and flats is calculated according to how many *tatami* mats they can contain. Every activity within a home or building takes place on a *tatami* mat. Because there are no chairs or beds, the outside is viewed from either a standing position or a sitting position on the floor. Sitting cross-legged on a veranda brings one closer to the

earth and helps the mind fall into step with the rhythm of the breeze as it rustles the leaves in a nearby bush.

The construction of temples was influenced by the custom of rulers to become monks on retirement, or to bequeath their private residence to a Buddhist sect. This partly explains why Kyōto has so many Buddhist temples. During the Heian period, when it became the new capital, it was planned on a grid system with areas progressively divided up. In this way, all levels of society were allocated an area that corresponded in size to their status. This obviously had an effect on building styles and the development of the garden. The larger plots, which were for people of high social standing, were about 1.4 hectares (3.5 acres) square, whereas the poorest people had little more than an alleyway or courtyard in which to make a garden. Whatever the size of the plot, it was usually contained within earth or clay walls, so that it became a quiet and more refined than the colourful Chinese style. Chinese- or Shinden-style mansions had wooden shutters to cover doorways, and cushions on the floor. The Japanese replaced the heavy wooden shutters with lighter paper-filled panels and covered entire floors with *tatami* mats. This resulted in a more flexible division of interiors; as the paper panels were easy to put aside they also allowed entire sides of a building to be opened to the outside. The new Shoin style of architecture remained popular for the next 400 years.

private place that held the whole world within its walls. Whether the space was large or confined, the Japanese designer was able to create a garden that represented the whole of nature in a carefully thought-out way.

Chinese or Shinden architecture was imported by Japanese aristocrats and is associated with large, south-facing, symmetrical buildings that had smaller buildings on either side connected to it by corridors. The front garden invariably boasted a pond of some sort with rocks representing Mount Hōrai or Mount Sumeru, which was the mythical centre of the Buddhist world, making the pond of primary importance. This affected the architecture of the garden because paths, miniature mountains and symbolic woods were of secondary importance and so were positioned after the pond had been constructed. The Heian period saw this Shinden style develop into a unique Japanese style of architecture that was

This style of garden design and architecture evolved further as a result of the conversion of the Kameyama Palace in the Arashiyama district of Kyōto, to a Zen temple, Tenryūji, by Musō Sōseki (see pp. 11 and 60). Instead of the garden being designed to be seen from a pond or paths set within it, the emphasis here was on viewing the garden from a seated position, usually from the abbot's *hōjō*. Musō Sōseki saw the garden as a teaching aid for Buddhist monks, who were supposed to contemplate the spiritual meaning woven into the area that could be viewed. In this way, gardens became quiet places in which to contemplate rather than spaces for the wealthy to play in. Shoin-style architecture evolved from this period, deriving its name from an alcove constructed in a perimeter wall for reading and writing. This change in the emotional use of the garden pervaded Japanese society, and it is still traditional for the man of the house to change from his business clothes into

a more casual style of dress on returning from work, and then spend time alone in the garden. Having calmed himself, he would then join his family.

One of the greatest differences between Shinden and Shoin architecture is that Shinden temples and residences were approached from a gateway south of the main hall. The area between the outside wall and the hall had the character of a courtyard, and gardens were not created in this space. Moving the place of entry to one side of the main hall made the courtyard space available as a garden. There is a sense of value connected with an enclosed space, and a challenge to make it seem larger while at the same time harmonizing it with the rooms adjacent to it. The 'windows' of temples

tsubo and in doing so lend its name to the garden owner. The appearance of these small spaces could be altered by placing seasonal-flowering pot plants in them. During the Edo period, the *tsubo* became symbolic of Japan's attitude to the world, as she effectively cut herself off from all western contact. Everything a gardener needed lay in this confined space, mirroring Japan's belief that she had no need to look beyond her boundaries because all she needed she could provide for herself.

and residences were large and powerfully geometric; they were often created by sliding one or two partitions to one side, so that the view to the garden was from floor to ceiling on one or two sides.

Japan is still influenced by its historical past; today many shopkeepers live behind their shops, and for a garden have what is little more than an inner pathway surrounded by buildings. These areas are known as *tsubo* gardens and are highly restricted, contemplative spaces similar to the corners tucked between the various many buildings attached to a palace in the Heian period. In the *Tale of Genji*, which was written at that time, we are told how one plant would dominate a

These viewing gardens were designed to be attractive all year round. To make a space appear larger, horizontal lines were used to layer it. By creating a foreground, a middle ground and a background, a sense of distance was achieved. In the West, small objects are usually placed in the foreground, but in these gardens nature was replicated by placing the largest object closest to the front of the garden. Small objects were placed in the background to suggest distance and space. Objects were also placed on an imaginary diagonal line to achieve a sense of distance. Because diagonal lines are inherently dynamic and create a visual tension, these small gardens became strongly three-dimensional. This in turn balanced the positive character of the adjacent room.

Today, many *tsubo* are designed with some reference to the tea garden that reached its cultural peak in the Edo period. Their character is similar in that they both often have gentle, low, light levels and are long, narrow and often

damp. Zen monks introduced the practice of tea drinking to Japan from China where it was a social and spiritual affair. The drinking of tea as a religious ritual began in China during the Sung dynasty (960–1279), when it was discovered that monks were able to meditate more effectively after drinking whisked green tea. This ritual was used to honour Bodhidharma, who was thought to have discovered the merits of tea, and took place in front of an image of him placed in a recess.

The shogun Yoshimitsu, who built the Golden Pavilion in 1397, is known to have held tea ceremonies there. It is thought that he used the ceremony as an opportunity for serious discussion of the merits of his latest Chinese artefacts. Not long after this, a country-bred monk at the Silver Pavilion, named Shuko (1423–1502), devised a tea ceremony that encouraged calmness, politeness, purity and a refined manner, in a building that is thought to have been fairly rustic. As with all rituals, time has shaped the tea ceremony, which in turn has influenced the design and construction of the tea house and garden.

In the Heian period, the tea ceremony was a contemplative ceremony in strong contrast to the fabulous extravagance of the Heian court. The ritual was further refined by the great tea master Sen no Rikyu (1521–91), who believed that rough country-style pottery would be more in keeping with the subdued atmosphere of the tea house than the finely glazed Chinese-style pottery. For this reason he commissioned a revered tile maker, Chōjirō, to produce pottery that had an irregular shape, decoration and glaze. This asymmetrical pottery was known as *raku* ware and came to epitomize the spirit of the Japanese. Rikyu built his own tea house, a small cedar construction with compacted earthen walls. He placed different-shaped papered, windows above the seated guests' heads so that the world outside could not be viewed. The entrance was a hole about 0.6 metres (2 feet) square, which came to waist height. This *nijiri-guchi* made all guests aware of their bodies as they bent to wriggle through the opening. It also humbled the spirit, as every man became equal to the next no matter what his social status. As each guest entered the tea house, he was aware that he was addressing his spiritual needs and leaving behind his public persona.

The approach to the tea garden, or *roji*, was designed with the aim of preparing the guest for the ceremony that lay ahead. Visual markers were used at intervals in the garden as an aid to the emotional journey the participant would make from a busy materialistic world to one of tranquillity, timelessness and contemplation. At one time, pilgrims had travelled up mountain tracks to *wabi* thatched huts to meditate, and the narrow approach to a tea house was designed to evoke the same feeling of pilgrimage. Ponds and stone groupings did not feature in the early tea gardens, which were loosely planted with mostly evergreen plants in a sea of moss. Few flowering plants were used in the garden, although inside the tea house a single flower might be placed in the alcove that was used for displaying a beautiful object to be discussed.

Opposite:
This magnificent lacquered gateway does not overwhelm its surroundings as tall trees close by help it to meld with the arrangement of cloud-pruned shrubs below it.

The outer entrance gate to the *roji* was usually roofed, and was a powerful pointer that the guest should begin to prepare himself mentally for his visit to the tea house. The path might be constructed of randomly shaped paving slabs set in a zigzag fashion. This had the effect of slowing the guest's walking pace The *roji* was often divided into two areas, and in the outer area there was usually a small thatched or roofed open-fronted hut where guests could sit and wait to be summoned to the ceremony. Not far away was a privy or toilet with a group of rocks near by, one of which was basin shaped and filled with water for the guest to wash his hands in. Purification was, and still is, an important part of the Shintō religion, and by washing his hands in the *tsukubai* the guest was symbolically purifying his soul. A lantern placed close by was both decorative and practical. In the early days of tea gardens, lanterns were sometimes obtained from temples and so had a religious connotation.

Opposite:
This entrance is a
masterpiece of refined
and understated
design. Step-over
fencing is unobtrusive
but practical while the
straight path has been
made less austere by
the use of irregular-
shaped flagstones.
Trees and rocks placed
randomly give a
feeling of tranquillity.

The second part of the *roji* was divided from the first by a simple gate, *chu-mon*, that might be simply roofed. This was another visual prompt to the guest to leave his worldly concerns behind and to prepare himself spiritually. The symbolic significance of the second gate was sometimes emphasized by placing it on its own rather than in a wall or fence. The stepping stones, *tobi-ishi*, in the second area were undressed and laid haphazardly to evoke the atmosphere of a high mountain path. The Japanese noticed that stones reveal their beauty and subtle colours most when moistened, so before a ceremony the tea master would carefully clean and then wet them. *Tobi-ishi* were important for decorative reasons and as a means of helping the guest to clear his mind finally, for their wide spacing, wetness and roughness demanded all his attention if he were not to slip.

Near to the tea house, the guest would find a water laver, or *chozubachi*, or a second *tsukubai*, where he would again rinse his hands and mouth while standing on a specially placed flat stone. Another flat stone was set by the *chozubachi* to give the guest an opportunity to set his own lantern down while he purified himself. A stone lantern set close at hand would add height and a decorative touch. Not far from the *tsukabai* was a small hole in the ground known as a *chiriana* originally a dust hole to receive the dirt sweepings from the tea house, it came to be a symbolic receptacle for emotional rubbish.

The tea master would stand on another specially placed stone to greet the guests to the rustic tea house, which often measured only three *tatami* mats. The entrance was often a small hole, which required everyone entering the small room to bend double. By making guests enter through such a restricted space, the interior was made to feel larger than it actually was.

The architecture of the tea house elevated the importance of unadorned natural materials, so that the Japanese came to value the rich patina of undressed wooden structural supports in domestic architecture. As Japanese architecture became more asymmetrical, it relied on dynamic angles and planes composed of different woods that were prized for the beauty of their grain. Since the tea ceremony traditionally took place in a simple, small space, modern Japanese sometimes create a tea ceremony room at the top of their houses, the journey up the stairs to reach it replicating the mountain pathway of pilgrimage.

A simple path of irregular-shaped stepping stones is all that is required to harmoniously link a dry rock and sand garden with a more verdant area.

Paths

Paths in the western world can be symmetrical or asymmetrical, whereas in Japan the only area that would be treated symmetrically would be close to a major Buddha hall. Symmetrical paths did not fit with the Japanese concept that a garden should be a copy or miniature version of natural scenery, and had no place in the more abstract *karesansui* gardens. With the development of Shoin-style architecture and gardens, there was less need for paths to be purely functional. Shinden gardens had been created for richly clad aristocrats to walk on in a leisurely way while enjoying the peach blossom and reciting poems. For these reasons, paths needed to be safe to walk on while also being visually attractive. Once gardens became places of contemplation and quietness, they tended to reflect the rough naturalness of a mountain track.

In some public Japanese and American gardens, concessions have had to be made with regard to the texture and style of the pathways used. This can be seen at the Golden Gate Park Japanese garden San Francisco, where more than a million visitors make quick tours of the garden; paths here have to be safe to walk on while being shaped in the Japanese tradition, rather than being entirely constructed in the Zen style. This also applies to domestic gardens where the owners may be unsteady on their feet.

Not many Japanese garden paths will run in a straight line from one point to another. Mythology might give the reason for this as being that evil spirits travel in straight lines, so a path that curves, forks or zigzags confounds bad forces. Anyone who has inherited a garden that is divided down the centre by a hard, straight, concrete path will have felt the negativity of such a design. A straight path has a hard, unrelenting nature that compels the walker to pass quickly along it. There is no invitation to stop and linger along the

way to admire the dew clinging to a leaf edge, or to look deep inside the throat of a rhododendron flower. Walking quickly along a narrow, straight path gives the walker little opportunity to slow down and emotionally unwind; instead, he or she continues to carry all the negativity collected during the day.

Because it was important that paths were visually appealing, they were designed in a multitude of styles, and still are. Irregular-shaped paving slabs or square, concrete slabs might be set in a sea of pebbles; irregular-shaped slabs might be set in a crazy-paving style, and 'poem-card stones' (see p. 128) could be interspersed with gravel and pebbles or laid with square, concrete blocks and pebbles. A Zen path is an opportunity for the designer to show off his or her skills in an enduring way.

As soon as a path has a bend or curve put into it, a sense of naturalness is created. A path that bends and twists takes the walker on an exciting journey. Designed with care, a path in even the smallest of spaces can impart a sense of making a strange journey to an unknown destination. The zigzag path of the tea garden took longer to traverse than if it had gone directly from one point to another. Such a path gives the illusion of space, and this is heightened when evergreen shrubs are planted thickly along it to obscure the view ahead partially. At the beginning of the path, there is no way of knowing the length of the journey ahead, and this creates a feeling of anticipation. When shrubs surround a path, there is a sense of privacy, seclusion and mystery, three emotions that many adults have little opportunity to experience. A small garden can be made to seem longer by taking a path around a small group of shrubs, which gives the walker an opportunity to make a personal choice to lengthen his journey or not.

At the ancient Zen temple of Tōfukuji, the Fumonin garden is bisected by a straight path that runs from the gateway to the founder's hall, or *kaizando*. There is a pond garden to the right of the path and a *karesansui* garden on the left. Harmony and a sense of balance have been created by these three design elements, which are overlooked by the powerfully dynamic *kaizando*. This balance has been achieved by making each element as beautiful and as complete in itself as possible. The path is edged with long,

1 **Plover design path**
2 **Wild geese design path**
3 **Path with dividing stone**
4 **Single stone path with stones set at angle**
5 **Flagstone and pebble**
6 **Flagstone**
7 **Paving stones and gravel**
8 **Edging stones, paving stones and gravel**
9 **Poem-card *nobedan* path**
10 **Rough, random stone path**

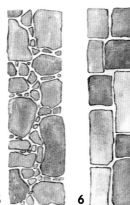

1   **2**   **3**   **4**

5   **6**   **7**   **8**   **9**   **10**

flat, paving slabs with three straight edges are sometimes laid with flat stones a third of their size that have one straight side. The straight edges will be set to the edge of the path to define its boundaries, while the broken edges allow small stones to be embedded in a random fashion around them. A path composed in this manner has a strong personality without appearing uncompromising in its rigidity. By weaving three different paving substances together a natural atmosphere is produced.

narrow sections of stone and the wide spaces between them are almost filled with large, geometrically shaped, undressed flagstones. The spaces between the blue-grey flagstones and the brown-tinged edging stones have been filled with small, flat-topped cobbles that vary in colour from grey to fawn, so pulling the three textures together. When the path is wet, the colours spring into life and bring a vibrancy to it that balances the moss-covered ground to the left, in the *karesansui* garden, and the low, clipped shrubs surrounding the pond and rocks to the right. The path is purposeful, and because it has been treated with Zen care and respect it is not flat or dull.

Flat, continuous paths have a refined, sophisticated air and can be of an intricate design incorporating stones of several different shapes and styles. This creates a path that is full of textural qualities, and which becomes a thing of value and beauty in its own right. Large,

Formal paths, or *nobedan*, were at times composed of stone slabs of varying geometric styles. The guiding design principle when laying strongly geometric paths was to lay each slab so that at least one of its sides was laid beside two slabs that were abutting each other. This rule ensured that the design was asymmetric while also being highly controlled. Paths of this type appear highly contemporary because they give the impression that the space is uncluttered and quietly dynamic. A *nobedan* might contain straight-sided, oblong stones similar in shape to the cards on which poems were written in the Heian period, so that they were known as 'poem-card stones'. A *nobedan*, or poem-card path, reflected the refined style of the building close at hand and unified it with the garden.

Zen practitioners appreciated that even a short journey down a path could have an effect on the mind and spirit. They believed that the posture one adopted while walking was important, and indeed

it is hard to feel melancholy when walking as though an imaginary string attached to the top of one's head were gently drawing one's posture straight. Where appropriate, walkways would be smooth to allow a lifting of the spirit and a feeling of lightness to flow into the walker. At other times, the pathway would be of a rough character that would require the walker's attention.

Rustic paths of single stones set apart were hugely popular in Japanese gardens because they were usually constructed from undressed stones. This gave the designer an opportunity to choose the most handsome stones possible, stones that were characterful and of a good colour that would become magical when glistening with early morning dew. These stones were usually flattish and of an irregular shape. The thicker and more raised above the ground, the more the walker had to take note of where he placed his feet. This was a Zen ploy to

Opposite:
A Mediterranean
climate has not
prevented the owner
of this plot from
creating a Zen
garden. Rocks, stones
and gravel blend
happily with Wisteria,
bamboo and the grey
leaves of Senecio and
Dianthus.

laid with its long edge going from one side of the path to another, could instead emphasize the length of the path by being placed lengthways on. Single-stone paths were laid mainly in one of three styles, but in each style the rocks were laid with their long edge at an angle to the next. The simplest-shaped path to make was one that gently curved; this gave the garden designer the chance to create an air of mystery by planting evergreen shrubs beside it that tantalizingly obscured the path's destination.

induce walkers to empty their minds of daily thoughts and move closer to the desired 'no-mind' state. The stones might appear to be randomly placed at first, but great care and attention was paid to how one stone related to the next and to the overall impression that they created. If most of the stones were the same shape and size, they might be laid in groups of two or three, interspersed now and then with a single stone of a different shape. The strata and natural direction of the stone would be taken into consideration, so that the dynamics of the path could be tweaked every now and then by placing one in the opposite direction from the one it seemed to dictate. This meant that a broad stone, which would normally be

The second style of path was symbolic of the plover's flight pattern, in which one bird leads a flock flying in a tight zigzag formation behind; a plover-style path might have stones grouped in twos and threes in order to mimic the plover's flight groupings. The third type of path was a much looser zigzag one, intended to mirror the flight of wild geese. Geese have a much wider wingspan than the smaller plover, which causes them to fly in a more spaced-out way. Both these styles of path were used in tea gardens to create an illusion that the path was longer than it actually was. It also introduced liveliness to the garden, which remained visually similar all year round.

Paths comprised of single stones could be made to weave among groups of rocks or plants, and could be continued through a stream and on to the opposite bank. Unspoken signals could be given to the walker to stop and admire a view or planting by placing a 'pausing stone' at

the viewing point. A 'pausing stone' was broader than the majority of the stones, and set slightly above its neighbours so that the walker could stand with both feet together to gaze at a hallowed rock or at verdant moss growing around a lichen-covered tree stump.

Another signal was given when a path was about to divide, by placing a broader stone in the ground. This dividing-stone gave the walker an opportunity to stand and debate which direction should be taken. 'Dividing' and 'pausing' stones in effect broke the monotony of a path consisting of stones of a similar shape and size, and introduced an element of interest and naturalness to the path – no mountain track would be of a uniform width and smoothness. A large stone was sometimes positioned at the beginning of a path immediately outside a building, and garden shoes left on it for visitors to put on, because they would have been shoeless inside the building.

Walls and screens

The pactice of mindfulness involves giving just as much attention to 'insignificant' things as to what we generally consider important things, and this applies to every aspect of garden design. A wall serves several purposes that it is important to consider before planning one of your own. One of the most important services they provide is to slow down gusts of wind; another is to provide privacy and a feeling of seclusion and security.

Anyone who has lived close to hills and mountains knows that wind can rush down a hillside to buffet savagely plots that nestle at their feet. A solid wall gives some protection to plants growing near by, but it is even more effective against wind if trees are planted at intervals alongside it. This creates an irregular barrier that slows wind down even more, while also providing a windbreak that harmonizes with the surrounding landscape.

In temple gardens such as Zuihoin, Ryōgenin and Daitokuji, clay walls topped with attractively shaped roof tiles are an integral part of the gardens design. The clay walls in Zen temple gardens' are either left a natural earth colour or are white, and are usually roofed with tiles that can be of a decorative nature. Where they surround a *karesansui* garden, they reinforce the feeling of peace and solitude that is evoked by a sea of sand and rocks. The eye is not distracted by a view beyond the arrangement of rocks, so beneficial contemplation can take place. White walls surrounding a *karesansui* garden act as a continuation of the designer's canvas, and this is fully appreciated in autumn when one acer, planted near the *hōjō*'s entrance becomes a flaming red.

Solid boundaries give a secure feeling to a garden but can be visually hard on the eye. The Japanese often created boundaries that were constructed of rocks up to a height of 1 metre (3 feet), with a further 1.5 metres (5 feet), of green, clipped hedging. Not only is this gentler on the eye, the two different textures of the stone and the shrub add greater interest to the garden. Many temple gardens have hidden boundaries in order to disguise the true size of the garden. This was achieved by banking earth up around the perimeter of the garden and planting it with shrubs to give additional height and thus break up the skyline. In North America, banks of earth, or berms, are made in the same way and act as a good sound barrier in noisy areas.

However, in an urban plot, earth should only be banked up where the retaining wall is strong enough to hold the additional weight, and where it will not cause damp problems for neighbours.

Open fences allow a view through to the area beyond while providing a physical boundary. In Japan, they tend to be made out of planks of wood or bamboo poles. In a tea garden, the fence dividing the entrance garden from the tea house garden was often constructed of bamboo. A *yotsume-gaki* is a bamboo lattice fence of a medium height, supported at either end by a wooden support. Because bamboo grows wild in Japan, this gives a natural feel to a garden. This is not the case in the West, and it might be more effective to construct a fence in the same way as a Japanese bamboo fence, but

Some dividing fences are constructed of bamboo stripped of its leaves and packed tightly together to make a solid wall. In the West, a similar wall could be constructed from hazel or birch branches, although a huge amount would be needed. Willow is available in different earth tones and has the restrained character loved by Zen garden designers; a good willow-weaver should be able to make a fence that has a geometric nature more in the Japanese style than in the usually less stylized western fence.

An ugly brick wall that has a dead feeling to it could be disguised with a lattice bamboo fence placed a little in front of it, which would suggest that an area lay behind it. A solid, wooden-plank fence or a continuous bamboo screen would completely disguise it and at the same time lend a natural air to an enclosed space. Replacing or covering hard manufactured materials with natural wood breathes life into an area and makes it more congenial.

The desire to create a harmonious environment led the Japanese to design a graceful, open type of fence known as a sleeve fence. The main portion of the sleeve fence is of an open-weave design, and it is the framework that gives this fence its name. Bundles of bamboo, bracken or bush clover are used to edge the fence, and this is sometimes curved gently from the top far corner down to ground level, or from the top far corner to just above the near-side corner. This imitates the shape of the wide sleeves of traditional Japanese costume. Sleeve

using plant material local to the garden. In Europe and Northern America, this might be by using hazel, chestnut, cedar or willow poles; these have a more subdued colouring than bamboo, which can appear too strident in the gentle light of the northern hemisphere. In this way, the garden would sit well in the local landscape just as a Zen garden does in its original environment. A willow- or chestnut-pole fence can be made in the same way as a bamboo one, and given the same *wabi* personality, by criss-crossing the poles and tying them with equal lengths of coarse black string, knotted with love and care.

Bamboo is often used in conjunction with wooden boards, and this creates a strong, geometric character that brings additional interest to an area, especially a shady corner where few plants are able to thrive.

fences are used when a boundary needs to be suggested and implied rather than enforced, as they are a gentle way of separating one area from another within a garden.

Gates were made in a similar way to a fence. An entry gate might be of solid planks of wood with no view through, but a gate set within a garden would often be of a simple lattice design. An important inner gate would be tall and roofed in thatch or bamboo, and the doors might be of single bamboo poles placed vertically in a wooden frame. The size would denote that an important area was being approached, while the view through it beckoned the visitor to enter. In this way, the emotions of the visitor were acknowledged and respect was paid to the garden owner.

When, just as they are,

White dewdrops gather

On scarlet maple leaves,

Regard the scarlet beads!

Ikkyu, Zen Poems

ORNAMENTS

Creating interest and beauty

Lovingly chosen ornaments Zen gardens nearly always contain ornaments thoughtfully introduced to enhance their atmosphere. They are used for symbolic purposes, as focal points and to humanize the garden. A water basin is a visual reminder of the need to cleanse oneself and to cast aside mundane thoughts; for this reason basins are placed at the entrance to the tea garden or near the tea house. Lanterns are often highly decorative and usually placed as an accent to a pathway or beside a pool or stream, so that their warm, flickering flame can cast a gentle glow on the black surface of the pool at night. A carved Buddha tucked among a camellia's glossy leaves reminds the visitor that there is a higher plane of existence than they have yet attained, and that this should be respected.

Decorative wrappings placed around shrubs and trees during the harsh winter

Ornaments and their surroundings

The greatest difficulty westerners have to face when planning a Japanese garden is the architecture of their home. In Japan, gardens are so completely relaxing and tranquil because they are not at odds with the architecture of the buildings that lie within them or are close by. The westerner has to be careful not to create a garden that sits unhappily in its surroundings and feels incongruous and alien, for then it will not be relaxing and inviting to any visitor.

months demonstrate the warmth of Buddha's love, which regards all plants as being of equal importance.

The very act of carefully placing a loved object in a garden introduces a gentleness to it. An object that means something special to the garden owner and has touched their heart has a good aura surrounding it. This intangible element is an important one in the garden because it beckons the visitor to step into the plot and to enjoy it. The human eye relays hundreds of visual messages to the brain very rapidly, and these in turn guide the emotions. It is therefore vitally important that any garden ornament be chosen with care and be loved by the garden owner. It is no good buying an ornament because 'it will do'. Far better to wait until one is found that asks the gardener to take it home. An ornament should give a frisson of pleasure each time it is looked at, for, when this happens, the gardener treats the area surrounding it with love and care to the benefit of the whole garden.

Ornaments have the power to tip the balance of a garden from one which feels authentic and enticing to one which has almost a theme park character. Some designers might like to think there are rigid rules that should be followed when placing an ornament in a Zen garden, but a Zen monk would probably declare that there are no rules. This is because following a rule could result in less harmony and tranquillity, which are the very objectives of a Zen garden. What feels right should be the guiding principle. In Japan, it might be traditional to place a lantern or water basin near the entrance to the garden, but in the west, the style of the house may be so completely different from the clean lines and natural wooden materials used in a Japanese building, that a lantern or water basin might lose all of its charm when placed near alien architecture.

If the garden owner has a house that does not harmonize with a Zen garden, he or she has two options to overcome this difficulty. In a small town garden, where space is at a premium, he or she can plan a garden that gently unfolds down the length of the plot. At the top of the garden, there might be a patio or decking with chairs for relaxing in. If pots containing bamboo and shaped shrubs are placed around this area, the visitor will be visually prepared for the treat that lies ahead. The character of the pots used is important because it is this that helps to counterbalance the simplicity of the planting scheme. Terracotta containers are associated with western gardens and should not be used; there are many glazed and frost-proof Asian pots on the market that are beautiful in themselves and which suit unassuming plants such as hostas, *Helleborus Orientalis* or *Ilex Crenata*. Brightly coloured annuals should not be used as they do not have a subdued personality and are therefore too strident for a Zen garden.

Below:
A lichen-encrusted urn
adds a timeless quality
to a planting of
predominately green
shrubs, while also
acting as a gentle
focal point.

At some distance from the building, a screening of shrubs could be planted that would break up the outline of the house when viewed from the end of the garden. Once past the shrubs, the garden could be more strongly oriental in character, and lanterns and water basins could be placed in suitable positions. In this way, the visitor would be gradually led into a purely Japanese garden. This design strategy recalls the mountain path that took the pilgrim from an urban sprawl to a remote and simple shrine.

The alternative to this approach would be to make a Japanese garden within a self-contained area fenced off from the rest of the garden. The difficulty that can arise with this solution is that the visitor may undergo an emotional and visual shock on entering a style of garden that is outside his or her previous experience. With time, though, the Zen garden would become familiar and the garden owner and visitor would then be mentally prepared to make the emotional leap from a known western environment to

Heian period, Japanese aristocrats enjoyed moonlight parties in the large pond gardens that were then fashionable, and presumably they would have carried brass or paper lanterns to enhance their enjoyment. The subtle light cast by a lantern on peach or plum blossom would have been valued by the people of this period. This appreciation of moody lighting is still evident in modern tea gardens, which are lit by lanterns at night, although candles have replaced the oil or tallow lights of the past.

a different world. Once this state of expectation was achieved, the garden would affect the garden owner or visitor in the same way as the experience of going to a regular place of worship. They would visit the garden at the direction of their spirit whenever they felt the need to settle themselves emotionally and spiritually.

Lanterns

Lanterns were popularized by tea masters during the Middle Ages, when they were used to light the path to the teahouse at night. Prior to this, stone lanterns had been found in temples, usually outside the Buddhist hall, lighting pathways and doorways or acting as memorials. It is thought that the first stone lanterns were imported from Korea, as were other artefacts with a Chinese theme. There are Chinese paintings of the Eastern Han period (AD 25–220) that depict courtiers sailing on a great lake in boats festooned with paper lanterns . Certainly, during the

The light produced by a lantern has a different quality from that of an electric light, and is more in keeping with a garden. The flicker of a natural flame makes shadows lengthen and shorten, adding a mysterious, magical touch to the smallest of plots. This is more pronounced if the garden is in an area devoid of street lighting, with only a silver moon and stars to compete with. Stone lanterns are now considered more decorative than practical, but it is much more enjoyable to sit at night in a garden that is lit by candlelightrather than lightbulbs, and if a lantern is used there is more likelihood of it being placed in an authentic Zen position. This in turn helps the garden to feel well designed and inviting.

Whether the lanterns in a garden are to be functional or not, they should be placed where they would usefully illuminate an area, such as at the beginning of or at a bend in a path. In tea gardens, lanterns were traditionally placed near a water laver so that guests could see to wash their hands, should the tea ceremony take place at night. By the end of the nineteenth century, they were very much a part of the design of domestic gardens and were used to draw attention to a plant or rock grouping. They were never positioned on their own but always as part of an intricate rock or plant arrangement. Today, many small courtyard gardens have a lantern included in the overall design, as they are an opportunity for the owner to demonstrate his or her sense of style. The more ancient and moss covered the lantern, the better, as it is deemed then to have dignity and a good character.

Lanterns were originally simple affairs as they were often cut from one stone. As their different uses developed, they were shaped into many styles, the more ornate being reserved for elaborate ceremonies. Most consisted of a pillar of stone supporting a box with open sides; once the oil or taper had been lit inside the fire box, paper was placed across the windows to prevent the flame being blown out. Early tea masters borrowed lanterns from nearby temples, but as time went on lanterns became permanent fixtures within the tea garden and many tea masters designed their own lanterns.

One of the most dramatic in appearance is the legged-harp lantern. It has two curving legs set widely apart so that one is placed in a pond and the other on the bankside. In this way, it acts as a strong, visual link between the water and the land. It has a small firebox in comparison with its wide top, which prevents any light from reaching skywards. It is named after the 13-stringed Japanese *koto* harp or zither. Planted lanterns are set firmly in the ground. The pedestal is upright and square, with a carved panel at the bottom; the firebox is square, with a roof that may turn up at each corner and is surmounted by a stone ball. There are different styles of planted lanterns, some having their pedestal set quite deeply into the earth to imply that it has been in that position for many years. Earth and foliage banked up around the base reinforces this impression, and creates a *wabi*, stable feeling to both the lantern and the surrounding area.

There are many different designs of the standard pedestal lanterns, and some have names that reflect their Buddhist or Shintō connections. For example, an attractive bell-shaped one is known as *nure sagi*, meaning 'wet crane standing in the rice fields with dew on its feathers'; a fond reminder that the crane symbolizes long life. Others may have deer carved on the firebox, because deer were thought to be mystical messengers, or carvings of the moon, sun or stars. These lanterns always appear to be standing on the ground rather than set firmly into it, and this gives them an air of expectation and alertness.

Lanterns that are designed to sit close to the ground have no pedestal and sometimes no plinth. These lanterns are placed among a group of rocks or on a raised mound so that they appear to be growing out of the ground. Their square, squat firebox reinforces this impression. This type of lantern should be sunk into the soil so that small-leafed plants can nestle around their sides to make them become at one with their surroundings. As they have no pedestal, and at the most sit on a low stone plinth, they have a more discreet personality than some other lanterns and are invaluable in a garden that is naturalistic in style.

Snow-viewing lanterns usually have a wide roof so that the firebox is protected from flurries of snow. These lanterns also have short legs set widely apart, to give the impression that they are boldly standing up the rigours of winter. Spirit houses are very like lanterns, being the same shape and size, but rings are placed on the roof to represent the five elements: earth, water, fire, wind and sky.

Opposite:
Japanese signposts
can be quietly
decorative. Here, the
fluid Kanji characters
contrast with the
smooth surface and
clean straight lines of
the post.

Pagodas

Another ornament seen in Zen gardens is what looks like a small pagoda. This is known as a *stupa* and in size can be anything from only a few feet tall to as tall as a building; they are usually made of carved stone and represent a sort of Buddhist reliquary, containing ashes or relics. A *stupa* can be designed in a wide variety of styles and this gives garden designers an opportunity to introduce a personal touch to a garden.

A *stupa* or pagoda is positioned in a garden to enhance a plant grouping or to create a visual point. Used as a visual point, they energize an area by adding a stable and attractive vertical element in contrast to the constant movement of surrounding shrubs and trees. They are best tucked among a group of evergreen shrubs so that only a portion can be glimpsed. Ideally, a pleasantly shaped branch should overhang a *stupa*, so that each complements the other. This creates a mysterious atmosphere, which is appealing. When a pagoda is positioned among flowering Japanese iris growing in a tranquil pond, it adds a dynamic element that strengthens the picture. This is because there is tension between a static object and one that moves. If it is placed beside an aged pine on the edge of a pond or stream, then its reflection will bring life and interest to the area, compensating for the lack of an abundance of flowers in the plot.

A pagoda may be difficult to find in the West, and when a source is found just one should be purchased, as only very large Japanese gardens would have had two or more. In a tiny courtyard setting, a small *stupa* can help to create the illusion of a *karesansui* or a mountain landscape. Care should be taken that the pagoda is in the same proportion to any rock arrangements as a life-size pagoda would be in a mountainous area. In this way, a very small pagoda, no more than 30cm (12 inches) high, can make large rocks seem like towering mountains.

Signposts

Another ornament used in a Japanese garden is a signpost. These can appear decorative to a westerner because they are sometimes made from a flat-sided piece of rock that in itself has an attractive dynamic power. Authentic signposts have characters, or *Kanji*, on them that are read from top to bottom. Where they serve a practical purpose, they are placed beside a path, often where it forks or changes direction, and used in this way, they are a visual reminder that the visitor is on a journey. Finding a signpost may prove hard, but if the search is successful, it could be used to create the illusion that the garden is larger than it actually is by standing it beside a false path, which seems to (but does not) lead to an unseen area that lies behind a thicket of shrubs. By positioning the signpost away from the main path and beside a lateral path, the impression is given that the side path is important and so must lead somewhere.

Opposite:
A handsome, weatherworn statue of an oriental man has been used to humanise and to provide additional interest to this simple planting of pines and shrubs.

All stone ornaments become far more attractive when they have lost their raw, new look, and painting a new object with natural yoghurt can help the ageing process along. The yoghurt will attract the spores of lichen and mosses, so that before too long the lantern or signpost will develop a mellowed appearance and give the impression that it has been in the garden for a very long time, so imparting a feeling of stability.

A stone ornament that should be used with special care is a stone Buddha-rupa. It should be remembered that a statue of a Buddha is a sacred object to many people, and for this reason any Buddha deserves great respect.

Placing one in a suitable corner of the garden will serve as a visual reminder of mankind's place in the world.

Carved Buddha-rupas come in many styles, but most have a gentle, reflective quality about them that can have a calming effect when looked on. If space allows, it would be best to design a special corner where meditation and contemplation can take place in front of the Buddha image. A sleeve fence or a screening of shrubs could be used to create a private space within a garden where it would be possible to sit undisturbed. A meditating stone, which is broad and flat, could be placed in front of the Buddha-rupa for sitting on. The larger the rupa, the further away the stone should be from it, so that the right space is created between it and the contemplator. If the rupa is small, he should be placed on a rock or in a niche in a wall so that he is not looked down on but looked up to slightly. Any planting scheme should enhance the effect of the Buddha-rupa but not compete for attention, as this would upset the meditator's concentration. The image should be the focal point of the area, whether it is nestling among lush leaves and rocks or placed against a relatively bare wall with gravel and rocks at his feet.

Making a personal space

The entrance to a private and personal area in a garden could be marked with a Shintō-style rope of twisted straw or hemp placed around a large, dynamic, upright rock, or around the stout trunk of an old tree. This would give the visual message that the area was a special spiritual place. Originally, Shintō ropes or cords were made of straw and were hung around

trees as well as rocks. The cords placed around trees were decorated with zigzag or folded strips of paper called gokei, which were symbolic of the many hands of the tree gods. Some Japanese Shintō shrines still honour their tree gods in this way, one of them being Futara san jinja. A favourite tree in a garden could be decorated in this way from time to time to draw attention to its grace and beauty, and to demonstrate the gardener's love of it.

Protective plant wrappings and supports

In Japan, infinite care is taken of trees and shrubs that could be damaged by severe winter conditions. The decorative, protective wrappings used around the trunks of trees are made from straw laid on them neatly lengthways, then held in place with black cord placed at regular intervals so that a decorative pattern is created. When the straw wrapping is continued up the trunk of the tree to the canopy, it is finished off with a neat, stiff, straw skirt. This is a highly attractive way of protecting plants in winter, because the

Below left:
A beautiful moss-
encrusted circular
water basin has been
tucked amongst
shade-loving ferns
to reflect the light
that filters through
tall trees.

straw coverings allow the shape of the shrub or tree trunk to be appreciated even when icy northern winds blast through a plot.

Sometimes it becomes necessary to support a tree, and in order to make the tree look as handsome as possible this is done by choosing and placing wooden props that become an integral part of the tree's design. Props are chosen to blend with the character of the tree that is to be supported, and are therefore quietly ornamental. A pine might be supported by poles that still have their bark on, or by smooth props that echo the colour of the pine candles. Wooden poles are usually set in the ground immediately beneath the branch that is to be supported, so that the pole is erect. A Japanese gardener would much rather retain an ancient, revered tree with the use of decorative wooden supports than allow it to become unsightly and misshapen as a result of weather damage.

Dark pebbles placed in the bottom of a water basin adds to its beauty in a subtle and alluring manner.

Water basins

Water introduces another dimension to a garden that is entirely beneficial (see pp. 35–52). Because it is one of the basic elements of life on earth, a garden that has even the smallest of water features feels more balanced and at ease with itself. A water basin can be positioned so that it reflects the sky above, unifying the earth and sky. Even in a subdued corner, it brings a shimmer of light that gently enlivens the area. The sound of tinkling water is alluring, and on a hot day will draw the visitor through the garden to discover its source. Since water symbolizes purity and is relaxing, it is no wonder that water basins became an intricate part of a Japanese garden.

Water basins are always ornamental in a Japanese garden, and although they are now generally associated with tea gardens, the idea of using water to purify one's spirit symbolically goes back to the first Shintō shrines. The concept of purity and impurity is a fundamental part of the Shintō religion. Early Shintō shrines were often in remote mountainous areas, and it is easy to understand how water running down a rockface into a small pool, close to a shrine, would become part of the rituals that surrounded the shrine. It is customary in tea gardens to rinse one's mouth and wash one's hands before the tea ceremony.

Japanese tea masters placed a group of stones, one of which was able to hold water, near the entrance of the garden and again close to the entrance of the tea house. The water basin was usually placed low down intentionally so that all guests, no matter what their social status, had to bend into a humbling position in order to purify themselves. This collection of stones was known as a *tsukubai*, although a *tsukubai* is often associated with a single natural rock that has had a smooth hollow carved into it to hold water. Sometimes a group of rocks might include a more refined artificial stone water bowl.

Water bowls are usually fed with water from a bamboo spout, or from a freshwater spring. Since they represent the act of purification, it is important that water is not allowed to stand for any length of time in them. When water stagnates, harmful bacteria build up in it that can cause the death of small birds; it also becomes a breeding ground for mosquitoes. Natural stone water basins are sometimes carved into the shape of an outstretched hand, and these are known as the Hand of Buddha. More commonly, they have a hollow in the centre, which may extend outwards to one side so that excess water can trickle down into another bowl placed slightly beneath it. With modern electric pumps it should be possible to take the water from the lower basin through a bamboo pipe or flume back up to the higher one – the tradition of setting water basins among rocks would facilitate this.

A *chozubachi*, or stone water laver, introduces a more sophisticated element to a garden that can be a welcome contrast to the roughness of the rocks used in it. Some are large, smooth-sided, rectangular stone objects that are about a metre high and have a masterful character. Some *chozubachi* are carved from stone so beautifully that they at first resemble a pottery basin. Tall, slender basins look lovely placed close to a veranda with a simple planting of camellias or bamboo nearby. Pieces of bamboo tied with black cord are often placed two-thirds of the way across the top of a *chozubachi* as a support for a water ladle. Square basins should always be placed at an angle to the nearby building so that a dynamic tension is created. A square or rectangular basin is sometimes decorated with a carving of the Buddha to act as a reminder that the clear, cool water within it is to be used with awareness and appreciation.

A more decorative water ornament is a deer scarer, which is constructed of two bamboo pipes. Farmers originally designed them to frighten deer and boar out of their fields, and from necessity they were made from simple pieces of bamboo and a rock, which would have been close at hand. A scarer needs to be placed near running water because a thin bamboo pipe is positioned with one end in the source of the water; this might be hidden by foliage plants. The other end of the pipe projects out from the shrubs so that it is immediately above the main bamboo pipe of the scarer. The main bamboo pipe is held loosely in a diagonal position by pins that pass through a piece of wood set in the ground, placed on either side of it, and into holes that are a little bigger than the pipe – this allows it to rock up and down. The end of the pipe nearest the water source is shaped like a ladle by hollowing out the first section of the bamboo. This allows water to be held in the pipe, but because it then becomes heavier than the opposite end it dips down so that the water spills out. When this happens, the opposite end tips down hitting a rock with a hard smack. The rock is known as the Sounding Rock. The sound the scarer makes is rhythmic like a Zen bell being rung, priests chanting or a clock ticking; it will sound more frequently if the water flows rapidly, but this could become intrusive.

A scarer is sometimes positioned so that the main pipe empties into a shallow basin that overflows on to a sea of pebbles set beneath it. There are many self-contained pebble water features on the market today that could easily be adapted to incorporate a scarer; these are usually powered by electricity (solar-powered ones are becoming available), which would enable the garden owner to stop the noise at night.

Another water feature that is occasionally incorporated into a Japanese garden, and in particular into a tea garden, is a well with a hoist and bucket. These are rustic and unassuming in character and most suited to a country garden. The well is composed of cut rocks, and when not in use is covered with a bamboo mat to prevent leaves and other debris falling into it. The ridged bamboo mat can also be used as a stand for a bucket. This is attached to a chain that hangs from an undressed tree trunk placed beside the well. Sometimes a well is given a thatched roof that makes it a strong garden

feature. In hot climates, the addition of a thatched roof would be a welcome source of shade and would invite the gardener to perch on the edge of the well to contemplate his or her domain.

Bonsai

It is only natural that the great love and admiration that the Japanese had, and still have, for plants should have led to the highly developed method of growing pot plants known as bonsai. From the twelfth century, this art crept into Japan from China, where it was adopted by people who already had a good working knowledge of growing plants in pots. Many aristocratic Japanese lived in apartments within palaces; these often had a veranda that overlooked a small courtyard where pot-grown plants could be used to draw attention to the time of year. The flowering peach or plum announced that winter was almost over and that spring was on its way. As it became fashionable to shape the trees in a garden to mimic those in Chinese scroll

paintings, so the art of bonsai developed. This skill made it possible for anyone to have their own miniature, ancient and revered tree. Bonsai growing is not Zen gardening, but for those with no garden it can offer the same contemplative rewards as the nurturing of a full-sized tree. The act of taking care of a precious plant frees the mind from thoughts of oneself; snipping minute leaves away from carefully shaped branches requires concentration and attention in the same way as raking gravel or trimming a bush.

There are nine basic bonsai shapes that can be achieved, and the one chosen is partly determined by the container that is to be used. The traditional container is an attractive shallow dish made from pottery with a decorative glaze; some trees call for a deeper dish. If a plum or peach is trained in an informal shape, it should be grown in a dish several inches deep, as should a tree that cascades, in order for the cascade to be fully appreciated. Semi-cascading trees also look their best when grown in a deeper container, and ideally the colour of the pot should provide a good background to the leaves of the plant.

A tree can be elevated in a shallow dish by being grown on top of one or two rocks that can represent a mountainside. Two styles that suit this treatment are the 'slanting' and 'windswept' shapes that are full of movement and character. A 'weeping' style gives a tree a reflective personality, while an 'upright' tree portrays a static character. Some trees are trained to have twin trunks, and these represent a

grove of trees. In bonsai growing, branches are trained into shape by being gently wired for perhaps three years. They need daily attention and should be regularly watered or misted so that they do not dry out. Every two or three years, they should be removed from their pot and roughly a third of their root system should be trimmed away (this should be performed in the spring). Before embarking on growing bonsai, it is well worth visiting a specialist grower, so that the right tree is chosen and a good understanding of its requirements is gained, in order to prevent it from dying.

Container gardens

In the Middle Ages, the Japanese also devised *karesansui*-style miniature gardens that were contained in a tray. Sand and rocks were arranged in an attractive shallow tray or dish to symbolize the ocean and Mystic Isles of the Blest, cranes or turtles. This is an idea that can easily be adapted to apartment living. A beautiful glass bowl could be filled with

An idea that may have developed from this in the West during the first half of the twentieth century was to plant a large shallow trough with miniature plants to create a tiny garden. A pagoda, bridge, rocks and a tiny, shallow water container were placed in the garden to give a sense of scale and to create a landscape similar to that on the willow-pattern plates that were also fashionable at the time. This is a truly delightful idea that could be copied by anyone so long as they have a small balcony or roof terrace.

sand and rocks collected from a seaside visit. A miniature tree could be made from a gnarled piece of wood found on a trip to a forest, and florist's lichen could be shaped and wired to the wood to mimic the abstract style of trees in Japanese gardens or as seen on willow-pattern plates. A thin piece of lichen could be placed around the base of the tree so that it appears rooted in the scene.

In the diaries of Richard Gordon Smith, which were written in the 1890s and 1900s when he was living in Japan, mention is made of container gardens planted at New Year. These often featured *Adonis amurensis* (a perennial with yellow flowers no more than 5cm, or 2 inches, across that open in spring before the leaves appear), an ancient pine, a small plum tree, a bamboo and the Heavenly bamboo, *Nandina domestica* (an evergreen or semi-evergreen shrub). All these plants were symbolic of the old year ending and the new year beginning.

Different plants would have to be used to suit the location; in very hot climates, heat-tolerant succulents could be used, while in damp, northern countries mosses and tiny ferns could be placed among some natural rocks. Average growing conditions would allow an infinite choice of plants to grow. Trees could be represented by *Salix Boydii*, *Salix helvetica* or *Betula nana*, and Japanese iris growing beside a pond could be replicated by *Sisyrinchium bellum*, which has tiny, sword-like leaves and purple flowers, planted beside a shallow saucer containing water. Most garden centres have a wide range of alpine plants, and staff can advise on the special needs of particular plants.

Today, it is hard to find old and attractive troughs, but there is often a good selection of shallow dishes suitable for growing alpine plants in. It is possible to make your own trough with a box of the required shape that is lined with plastic, then lined again with a mixture of 1 part of fine peat with 1¼ parts of fine cement to 3 parts of horticultural perlite or sand mixed with water. This should be of a manageable consistency so that it can be pressed around the edges of the box to a depth of 3–5cm (1½–2 inches). Remember to leave a hole in the bottom for drainage, and let the trough harden for three to five days. If you are making quite a large trough, it would be a good idea to line the box with fine-grade chicken wire to reinforce it, before pressing the mixture on to it. To age the outside of the trough, paint it with natural yoghurt.

A miniature garden is the most inspiring way of introducing a child to gardening. Creating a garden on a small scale gives children an opportunity to relate to plants that are of a similar size to their toys, and encourages them to take care of a plot of their own that is manageable and fun. With encouragement to practise Zen gardening on a tiny scale, a love of plants can be sown in the heart of a child that will grow and mature throughout his or her life.

Glossary and Bibliography

Akamatsu-ishi	red pine stone
Chiodori-kake	plover path
Chiriana	hole in the ground for sweepings found in tea gardens
Chōzubachi	water basin
Chū-mon	roofed gate
Gan-kake	goose path
Hōjō	Abbot's quarters
Hsein	immortal beings
Ichimatsu moyō	checkerboard design
Ikekomi gata	lantern planted or sunk into the ground
Jōdo	Pure Land
Kaizando	founders' hall
Kamejima	a group of rocks representing a turtle
Karedaki/karetaki	dry waterfall
Kareiki	an arrangement of white sand or gravel representing a pond
Karesansui	a garden scene that represents water with the use of sand and gravel
Koto-ji gata	two-legged harp lantern
Kutsu-nugi	shoe removal stone
Nijiri-guchi	small entrance hole in a teahouse

Nobedan	formal path
Qi	vital breath
Rigyō-seki	carp stone as part of a ryumonbaku
Roji	a narrow area leading to a teahouse
Roji-mon	entrance gate
Ryūmon	a waterfall known as a dragon gate
Ryūmonbaku	an arrangement of rocks making a waterfall that incorporates a ryumon
Sansui	Chinese style
Sanzon-ishi-gumi	three rocks representing the Buddha trinity
Shakkei	borrowed scenery, the scenery behind a plot
Shan shui	mountains and water
Shintō	Japan's native animistic religion
Shishi odoi/susu	deer scarer
Sode-gaki	sloping fence resembling the edge of a sleeve
Sosei	covered jetty area
Tatami	straw mat
Tobi-ishi	stepping stones
Tsuboniwa	very small area of garden
Tsukubai	basin for washing hands
Tsurujima	a collection of rocks representing a crane
Wabi	refined and subdued rustic taste
Yotsume-gaki	bamboo lattice fence
Yukizuri	rope tree snow guards

Baldock, John, *The Little Book of Zen Wisdom*, Element, 1994

Bancroft, Anne, *Zen*, Thames & Hudson, 1987

Davidson, A.K., *The Art of Zen Gardens*, Tarcher, 1987

Gordon Smith, Richard, *The Japan Diaries*, Viking Rainbird

Horton, Alvin and Crocker Cedric, *Creating Japanese Gardens*, Ortho Books, 1989

Keane, Marc, *Japanese Garden Design*, Charles E. Tuttle, 1997

Lowe, John, *Into Japan*, Salem House

McCullough, Helen (translator), *Genji and Heiki*, Stanford University Press, 1994

Nitschke, Gunter, *Japanese Gardens*, Taschen, 1996

Sawyers, Claire (Ed.), *Japanese Gardens*, Brooklyn Botanic, 1989

Scott, David, *The Elements of Zen*, Element, 1997

Seike, Kiyoshi, *A Japanese Touch for Your Garden*, Kodansha International, 1993

Shikubu, Murasaki, *The Tale of Genji*, Penguin, 1980

Shonagon, Sei, *The Pillow Book of Sei Shonagon*, Penguin, 1971

Slesin, Suzanne, *Japanese Style*, Clarkson Potter, 1994

Stanley-Baker, Joan, *Japanese Art*, Thames & Hudson, 1984

Stryk, Luycien and Ikemoto, Takashi (Eds.), *The Penguin Book of Zen Poetry*, Penguin, 1987

Index

acers 27, 32, 48, 92, 99, 100, 107, 108, 132
akamatsu-ishi 64
Amida Buddha (Amitabha) 9, 18, 28, 41, 41
Arashiyama 60
architecture 116-25
asymmetry 8, 45, 64, 69, 125, 126
azaleas 28, 46, 99, 104, 107, 109

balconies 87-8
bamboo 27, 32, 92, 112, 115, 116, 132, 134, 138, 150, 154
Bloedel Reserve, Bainbridge Island 82, 91
Bodhidharma 121
bonsai 153
'borrowed scenery' 28, 60, 66, 73, 79, 91
Bosatsu, Yakuo 28
brick 88, 92
bridges 24, 45-9, 51, 60, 154
Buddha 8, 21, 28, 60, 63, 64, 81, 84, 137, 138, 147
Buddha-rupa 147
Buddhism 8, 12, 16, 18
see also Five Mountain Buddhism; Gozan Buddhism; Pure Land Buddhism; Zen Buddhism

camellias 27, 107, 108, 137, 150
carp 22, 39, 60
carp stones 22, 39, 64, 66
cascades 40, 66
cherry trees 25, 103-4
Chikurin'in 46
chiriana 125
Chōjirō 122

chōzubachi 125, 150
chūmon 125
Como Ordway Memorial Japanese Garden, Minnesota 24, 40
Compton Acres, Dorset 25, 48, 107
container gardens 153-4
contemplation 8, 18, 49, 75, 82, 87, 126
cranes 16, 18, 41, 42, 59, 143

Daichiji 28
Daisen'in garden 18, 70, 79, 82, 83
Daitokuji temple 11, 18, 63, 79, 132
deer scarers 150
Deshima 81
designing a zen garden 107-9
dividing-stones 131
Doryu, Rankei 9
Dr Sun Yat-Sen Garden, Vancouver 56
dragon mythology 21, 22, 39
drum bridges 46, 48, 52

Egen, Kanzan 11
Eihōji 30, 31, 46, 52
enlightenment 18, 22, 46
Erinji 31

Fang-hu 16
fences 132, 134, 147
Feng Shui 9, 45, 56, 64, 92, 116
festivals 96
fish 49, 51
Five Mountain Buddhism 11
Floating Temple, Lake Biwa 39

Fort Worth Botanical Garden Center, Texas 45
Fumon pond garden 42

gates 116, 119, 122, 125, 134
geomancy see Feng Shui
Ginkaku-ji 39
gokei 147
Golden Gate Park, San Francisco 12, 31, 32, 40, 48-9, 126
Golden Pavilion, Kyōto 11, 22, 39, 40, 41, 64, 118, 121
Gozan Buddhism 11
grasses 28, 41, 46, 82, 96, 110, 112
gravel 8, 63, 74-93, 101, 153
ground cover 109-10, 112

Hanazono, Emperor 11
Hand of Buddha 149
Heian-Kyo see Kyo[-]to
Hiroshige, Utogawa 37
hōjō (abbot's quarters) 28, 30, 63, 76, 79
Horai, Mount 30, 119
Hōraito 11
Hōraito islands 28, 41, 64
Horaizan, Mount 41, 64
Hsien (Immortals) 16, 17

ichimatsu moyō 64
Imoko, Ono no 37, 39
irises 42, 45, 96, 99, 144, 154
Ise-Yatsuhashi shrine 22
islands (main reference) 40-42

Japanese Garden, Portland, Oregon 12, 21, 24, 25, 31, 40, 63, 83, 84, 103, 104, 107, 110
Jikoin 28
Jōdo Buddhism 11, 18, 42
Juraku-dai 12

Kameyama Palace, Kyōto 119
karedaki 24, 59, 63
kareike 24
karesansui (dry water garden) 11, 12, 22, 24, 28, 30, 73, 75, 76, 79, 81, 82, 91, 101, 127, 128, 132, 144, 153
devising 87-92
Katsumoto, Hasokawa 63
Kenchōji temple 9, 30
Kinkaku-ji, Kyōto see Golden Pavilion
Kokokuji garden 79, 82, 91
Kono, Motonobu 63
Koshōji Temple 41
kutsu-nugi 79
Kyōto 9, 12, 32, 63, 109, 116, 118

Lake Biwa, near Kyoto 39
lakes 12, 17, 30, 37, 39, 40-41, 45, 83, 104
lanterns 30-31, 122, 125, 137-40, 143, 145
lichens 24, 30, 42, 55, 60, 131, 147, 154
Loo Zi 56
lotus flower 28

Mahasattva, Prince 21
Mankōji garden 46
meditating stone 70
meditation 8, 12, 56

Mirei, Shigemori 64
Missouri Botanical Garden 45, 46, 82
moon 8, 27, 32, 76, 112, 140
mosses (main references) 27-8, 109-10
mountains 15, 16, 28, 31, 32, 37, 59, 79, 116, 118, 119, 144
Mountains of the Blest 30
Musaikyō bridge 46, 52
Myocho, Shuho 11
Myoshinji temple 11, 63
Myōzenji 24
Mystic Isles of the Blest 16, 17, 18, 27, 39, 41, 41, 59, 64, 110, 153

Nakaniwa gardens 81
Nara 9
nijiri-guchi 122
Nikka Yuko Japanese Garden, Lethbridge 65, 66
Nine Mountains and Eight Seas 18
'no-mind' 12, 21, 24, 56, 131
nobedan 128

Old Shūrinji garden 41, 46
olive trees 109
ornaments 136-55

pagodas 31, 144, 154
paintings
Chinese 18, 22, 25, 63, 140
ink 11, 60, 100
Japanese 25
scroll 11, 18, 21, 22, 25, 28, 41, 118, 153
pathways 8, 39, 51, 116, 119, 126-31, 139
pausing stone 131
pavilions 39, 84, 118
peach trees 24, 98, 153
pebbles 32, 35, 45, 51, 52, 56, 91, 115, 126, 150
P'eng-lai 16, 24
pines 24-5, 36, 41, 46, 52, 84, 101, 103, 104, 107, 144, 148, 154
plants (main reference) 94-113
plum trees 24, 25, 27, 153
poetry 25, 39, 45, 126
ponds (main references) 40-41
dry (kareike) 24
making 49, 51, 52
rocks in 73
pottery 122, 138
pruning 100-101, 103
Prunus 109

Pure Land Buddhism 11, 18, 18, 28, 41, 41, 42
Pure Zen 9
purification 122, 125, 149

raku 122
Reitōin garden 46
rhododendrons 103, 107, 108, 109
Rikyu, Sen no 122
rivers 9, 18, 37, 116
rock masters 59, 70
rocks (main references) 54-73
in abstract gardens 63-4
choosing and selecting 70, 73
positioning 69-70
representational 64-6
their place in contemporary gardens 66, 68
Three Buddha 11, 42, 52, 64
types 70
understanding 69
woven ropes 57, 59, 147
roji see tea gardens
Rokuonji 11, 22, 64, 118
rooftop garden 66, 70
Ryōanji 21, 24, 63, 76, 82, 83, 103
Ryōgenin 30, 132
ryūmonbaku 60

Saihōji, Moss Temple/Garden 11, 18, 27, 42, 49, 59, 109
sand (main reference) 74-93
sanzon 11, 24, 42
Sanzon-ishi-gumi 21
screens 18, 22, 116, 134

streams 9, 15, 32, 37, 45, 48, 49, 51-2, 66, 104, 107, 137, 144
dry 24, 63, 73, 104
stupas 31, 144
Sugimoto, Masami 65
Sui Yan Ti 37
Sumeru, Mount (Meru) 11, 18, 119
sun 32, 84, 100, 110
sutras 28
symbolism 15-33

Tai-yu 16, 17
Taizō-in garden 45, 63
Taoism 11, 16
tatami mats 118, 119, 125
Tatton Park, Cheshire 41
tea ceremony 12, 121-2, 125, 140
tea gardens (roji) 12, 30, 122, 125, 127, 132, 137, 140, 149, 150
tea houses 12, 48, 107, 122, 125, 137
tea masters 125, 143, 149
temple construction 118
Tenryūji 11, 60, 119
Tentoku-in temple 42
tigress fable 21, 63, 84
tobi-ishi 125
Tōfukuji garden 42, 64, 127
Tōkai-an temple 21, 81
Tokōji temple 9
tree gods 147
trees (main references)
blossom 103-4
decorating 147
protective wrappings 137-8, 147-8
pruning 100, 101
supporting 148
symbolism 24-5, 27
tsubo gardens 121
tsuboniwa 30
tsukubai 122, 125, 149
tsurujima 18, 42
turtles 16, 41-2, 59, 64, 70

verandas 84, 115, 118, 150, 153
Viburnums 107-8

wabi 30, 32, 48, 52, 63, 104, 122, 143
walls 132, 134
water (main reference) 34-53
water basins 137, 138, 139, 149-50

shakkei gardens 28, 60, 73, 79
Shinden architecture 119, 126
shingle 85, 91
Shintō 8, 9, 16, 18, 28, 30, 33, 56, 57, 76, 116, 122, 143, 147, 149
Shōden-ji, Kyōto 28
Shōhukuji monastery 22, 24
Shoin architecture 119, 126
Shonagon, Sei 25, 27, 30, 95, 96, 116
shoreline 42, 60, 81
shrines 8, 24, 30, 116, 147, 149
shrubs (main references)
flowering 104
protective wrappings 137-8, 147-8
pruning 100, 101
Shuko 121
signposts 144, 147
Silver Pavilion 121
Smith, Richard Gordon 154
snow 37, 60, 81, 96, 104, 143
soil 103, 107
Soko, Kogaku 18, 79
Sono Tsukuru Kami 22
Sōseki, Musō 11, 18, 59, 60,119
spirit houses 143
spirits 8, 45, 96
stepping stones 82, 125
stones (main references)
choosing and selecting 70, 73
pathways 128, 131
red pine 64
shoe removal 79

water laver 125, 140
waterfalls 30, 32, 33, 37, 39-40, 45
Dragon Gate 11, 22, 39, 60, 64, 66
dry 24, 63, 73
making 49, 51
wells 150, 153
Western Park 37, 39
Western Pure Land 18
wheeping cherry 103-4
willow 134
Wu, Emperor 17
Wu Ti, Emperor 28

Yin and Yang 9, 21, 25, 30, 56, 59, 87
Ying-chou 16
Yoshimitsu, shogun 11, 22, 39, 121
yotsume-gaki 132
Yuan-ch'iao 16, 17
yukizuri 104

Zen Buddhism 7, 8, 11, 60, 101
Zuihō-in 81, 132

Acknowledgments

I would like to thank my daughter, who thankfully has a degree in Japanese, for all her help and encouragement. A big thank you to Nancy Goldman who made my visit to Portland, Oregon, possible and to all those at the Japanese Garden of Portland and at the Japanese Garden in Golden Gate Park, San Francisco for their time and advice. Thank you to all the American Japanese gardens who kindly sent me information and The Japanese Garden Society of Great Britain. Finally, thank you to Clare Johnson, my editor, and the rest of the team at Pavilion.

The author and publisher gratefully acknowledge the following for permission to use the following extracts:

Pages 7, 15: Baldock, John, *The Little Book of Zen Wisdom*, Element, 1994
Pages 35, 55, 75, 95, 115, 137: Stryk, Lucien and Ikemoto, Takashi, *The Penguin Book of Zen Poetry*, Penguin, 1987

PICTURE ACKNOWLEDGMENTS

The Publisher should like to thank the following sources for their kind permission to reproduce the photographs in this book:

Arcaid Richard Einzig, *design* Artochenko 6, 120; Ian Lambot 2, 3; William Tingey 117.
Jonathan Buckley *design* John Tordoff 95.
Garden Picture Library Clive Boursnell 48; Rex Butcher 65, 93, 124; John Glover 105; Lamontagne 10, 74, 83, 133; Ron Sutherland 34, 53, 72, 90, 118.
Jerry Harpur 86; The Japanese Stroll Garden, Clifton, New York, USA 35; Ryoan-Ji Temple, Kyōto, Japan 5, 9, 58, 62, 75, 79, 129, 137, 145; *design* Terry Welch, Seattle 77, 80, 97, 152, 155.
Sunniva Harte Compton Acres, Dorset, UK 14, 20, 26; Mrs. Cummings, Riverwood, Portland, Oregon, USA 135, 148; Japanese Garden, Portland, Oregon 19, 25, 44, 85, 98, 101, 102, 142, 149; Japanese Garden, Golden Gate Park, San Francisco, USA 17, 31, 37, 61, 123, 141.
Andrew Lawson 151, Asticou Gardens, Maine, USA 126; Jojakko-Ji Garden, Kyōto, Japan 33, 67, 114; Private Garden, USA 23, 47, 55, 146.
Marianne Majerus *design* Peter Chan and Brenda Sacoor, Silverstream, Weybridge, Surrey, UK 89, 136; Herons Bonsai Nursery, Surrey, UK 68; The Japanese Garden, Clifton Notts. UK 41, 115, 130; *design* John Tordoff 29.
Clive Nichols 109; Honda Tea Garden, Chelsea 1995, *design* Julian Dowle and K. Ninomixa, 13, 49, 106; Little Coopers, Hampshire, UK 38, 50; Natural and Oriental Water Gardens, Hampton Court 1998 113; Netherfield Herbs, Suffolk, UK 15; *design* Thomas Nordstrom and Annika Ojkarsson 54; *design* Julian Treyer-Evans 7; *design* Gordon White, Texas, USA 139; Woking Borough Council, Chelsea 1993 87.
Steven Wooster 71; Ian Fryer, Christchurch, New Zealand 111; Isabella Plantation, Richmond, Surrey, UK 94 Eiji Morozumi, Sydney, Australia 43.